THE KING OF ASHES

The King of Ashes

John Barnie

GOMER PRESS
1989

First Impression—1989

ISBN 0 86383 537 6

*This volume has been published with the support of the
Welsh Arts Council*

*Printed by J. D. Lewis & Sons Ltd.,
Gomer Press, Llandysul, Dyfed*

Acknowledgements

'Cover Story' first appeared in *Living Blues*; 'Bread and Beauty', 'Never Forget Your Welsh', 'Across the Grain', 'The Janus County', 'The Shadow of Aberffraw', 'The Art of Puffing', 'Big Road Blues', 'Shot the Innocent Man', 'The City and Nature', 'Fault Lines', 'The Laureate and the Firm', 'Heroic Laughter', and 'The King of Ashes' in *Planet*; 'The Naming of Places', 'The Anglo-Welsh Tradition' and 'Brendan Kenelly's Cromwell' in *Poetry Wales*. 'Afro-American Music in Britain' and 'Robert Lowell's *History*' are previously unpublished.

My thanks to Helle Michelsen and Ned Thomas for their criticism.

Contents

Introduction

These essays and review-articles reflect a search for some kind of cultural identity. A hundred years ago my paternal grandfather emigrated from Caithness, leaving a society of crofter-fishermen for the eastern edge of the Monmouthshire coalfield where he worked as a packman for a Brynmawr draper. Later he joined the police force, serving in Abergavenny and various rural stations in what is now north-east Gwent. When he died in Monmouth in 1915 he had worked his way up to sergeant. My father was born in 1902 in the Old Gaol, Monmouth. His bedroom was the condemned cell where iron bars criss-crossed the one high semi-circular window, 'thick as the arms of a man'. He remembered tales of the last public hanging in the town, from an old man who had been a witness.

My mother's family were Fletchers from the Forest of Dean. They married into a family of Williamses who drifted into the Forest in the nineteenth century. My great-great-great uncle was Zephaniah Williams, the Chartist. I learnt of him as someone, almost, to be ashamed of. The text he wrote beneath a picture of the Crucifixion in his pub in Nant-y-glo—'This is the man who stole the ass'—would have scandalized both sides of my family, as it liberates me.

When John Henderson Barnie died suddenly, his youngest child, my father, was taken out of school and apprenticed to a grocer in Monmouth. In the early 1920s he worked as a grocer's assistant in Abergavenny, before setting up a sweet-shop in the town with a capital of £100. His six brothers and sisters were all shopkeepers or were married to shopkeepers. When he met my mother, she was an assistant in an Abergavenny shoe-shop.

So in two generations the family made the transition from subsistence farmers to tradespeople. This involved the mutation of the innate conservatism of the crofter into the political Conservatism of the *petit bourgeois*. It involved, too, the loss of religion. My grandfather had been a member of the Wee Frees in Scotland and settled for Congregationalism as the nearest thing in Wales. My mother's family were low-church Anglicans. My father and mother had a strict religious upbringing, but like all their brothers and sisters, abandoned it as soon as they could for tokenism. They had a residual sense of religion as something good for children, so that although they almost never

ix

went to church themselves, they expected me to go. In his later years my father believed vaguely in reincarnation, but would still have called himself a Christian.

Whatever culture had been brought by my grandfather from Caithness was lost to his children. What they absorbed in the 1920s and 1930s was the more genteel end of mass popular culture. The books in our house were *Lorna Doone, Ivanhoe* and *Best Poems of 1920* from my mother's days in the Girls' High School, my father's series of *Horse Racing Almanacs* and a Ready Reckoner.

My parents had vague notions about culture which included a belief that piano playing was a social accomplishment. I was put to it for five years with a piano teacher and at one time could read simple music, a skill I have totally suppressed. The ineffectual light-classical pieces I was coached through have also gone. I cannot remember the title of a single one. Playing the piano was a task on summer evenings, and whenever I sat down to it I felt I had wooden arms.

I learnt what music was when I heard the blues of Blind Lemon Jefferson and Huddie Leadbetter at the age of sixteen. I had never heard anything rhythmically exciting before, nor any songs that addressed real experience. Only then did I begin to understand my dissatisfaction with the sentimental masquerade of dance music on the radio, and with the lead-footed piety of nineteenth-century hymns in church.

In sixth form and at university I acquired slowly a knowledge of English literature. The poetry from *Beowulf* on was its centre and because this moved me, I accepted my teachers' conviction of its importance as *the tradition*, in the sense defined by T. S. Eliot in 'Tradition and the Individual Talent'. I did not realise at the time that mine was the last generation to receive a literary education based on such a notion, and almost the first in which it was made accessible to more than a handful of people below the middle class.

In the 1970s I taught English and American literature at Copenhagen University during a decade in which the idea of the tradition was not only challenged but destroyed. The tradition had been real enough but it depended on a *bourgeois* culture that lost its power base. The great attempt at a liberal education system for all foundered in the 1960s and 1970s, and with it the idea of the tradition. All this is well known, of course, but it was not clear to me then.

And after it, Post-Modernism. Instead of the tradition, a feast of traditions. For some years I was antagonistic to the term. Its lack of imagination—after Modernism, Post-Modernism—seemed a sign of cultural bankruptcy. It still does, for many of the 'cultures' and 'sub-cultures' jostling each other for attention are trivial and narrow, often with a strong bias against intellect and intelligence.

Yet I came to see grudgingly that my own experience was part of the phenomenon. My 'culture' was a self-created one, compounded of black American music, English-language poetry, natural history and in an ambiguous way, the literary culture of Wales. At each point on this personal compass I could talk to others, yet only in an incomplete way, with a part of myself. If I have had a few knowledgeable conversations about the blues, they have been with people for whom my other cultural compass points meant nothing. The whole, if I have succeeded in integrating it at all, is a private 'culture' and rarely communicable.

Yet how far is it possible to integrate such a magpie's collection that depended on the historical circumstance of my upbringing on the edge of Wales, and on chance? I have listened to the blues almost every day for thirty years, but the music can never be a part of me as it can for a black man or woman in Mississippi. And I can never feel at ease in Welsh-speaking Wales because I came at the language too late. In the Post-Modern world the pleasure of diversity is pursued in isolation cells.

Until recently I thought one thing could be depended on—nature. I thought this because in my childhood the foothills of the Black Mountains and the fields along the River Usk where I played, seemed timeless. Few people went there; nothing could change their beauty. Swallows, house martins and sand martins, whitethroats and blackcaps, would come back each year.

Now I have learnt a different truth. Outsiders have discovered the Black Mountains, have bought up the houses, turned the schools into adventure centres; the hills are patrolled by 'wardens'; pony trekkers, motorcyclists, hikers erode the grass tracks and disturb the quietness. The fields around the town are being lost to housing estates for the newly rich. The lapwings and curlews that bred there are gone; and along the banks of the Usk there are fewer sand martins that once bred in hundreds, fewer dippers, herons, common sandpipers, kingfishers. Even the green mass of the hills that seemed only to change with the seasons is being changed now by pollutants blown on the winds from the industrial towns to the west.

If nature cannot be depended on, what then? Beauty has been abandoned for profit and our ruthlessness seems to know no end. *Homo homini lupus est* was the Latin proverb. Man is a wolf to man. But man is a wolf to the Earth as well and we are afraid to look too deeply into his eyes now. These essays were written over the past ten years. They identify the cardinal points on one compass in the Post-Modern confusion. They attempt also a look in the mirror at the wolf we call man.

WALES

Bread and Beauty

R.S. Thomas does not have television and rarely reads a newspaper—sources of information which might seem essential for anyone who wishes to make political statements about Wales. Moreover his public utterances are bitter and uncompromising, made without apparent concern for what most would see as the real world of politics. This has caused some to ask whether he has a policy at all, for he makes no attempt to capture what might be a sympathetic ground among the English-speaking Welsh and English settlers. If politics is the art of the feasible then a policy must be flexible, able to adjust and make concessions in order to attract the widest support. To propound a policy in the face of indifference or widespread hostility is to fail. In mass democracy, policy must please a large section of the population or the party goes down.

By these criteria R.S. Thomas can hardly be said to have a policy, nor can he be taken seriously as a source of political thinking in Wales. But that, of course, is to accept the criteria—British democracy's version of *real-politik*.

There is another politics which perceives as its goal the realization of truth and which is prepared to go under rather than compromise that truth. 'What is truth'? the modern sceptic will ask. And in a world limited by human perception it is unknowable in any objective sense. It cannot be demonstrated, it can only be attested to in an individual's life. If enough people bear witness with him, that truth becomes revolutionary. If not, and the pull of society is against him, the individual ends in bitter isolation.

This notion of truth and its politics is Romantic in the historical sense. R.S. Thomas has never hidden his debt to the English Romantic poets—in his latest collection of poems, *The Echoes Return Slow*, Wordsworth, Coleridge, Byron, Shelley are frequent touchstones. His politics, too, is deeply marked by the ideas of these men, though in a more disguised form, for the immediate, observable influence on his thinking is Saunders Lewis. Nonetheless, like Shelley, R.S. Thomas is a confrontationist. Truth is not open to barter. Once seen, it must be pressed home without quarter to prevaricators, statesmen, balancers of fine weights.

This becomes clear in *Pe Medrwn yr Iaith* (If I Could Speak the Language)[1] which collects his most important essays and lectures in Welsh from 'Arian a Swydd' (Money and Position) published in 1946 to 'Undod' (Unity), the J.R. Jones Memorial Lecture given in 1985.[2] Some of these pieces, including 'Abercuawg' and 'Y Llwybrau Gynt', were published in translation in *Selected Prose* (1983), but together with his autobiography, *Neb, Pe Medrwn yr Iaith* is R.S. Thomas's most significant work in prose and establishes his importance to Wales as a thinker in the Romantic tradition.

In the world we live in, the word Romantic needs definition, for it is easy to dismiss it especially in a political context as implying impetuous and naive, or (remembering Wordsworth and Coleridge) reactionary, anti-industrial, anti-modern. R.S. Thomas's ideas derive from several strands in Romantic tradition and defy the crude categories of contemporary British politics. Some of his thinking is conservative in the literal sense of the term, making it possible to hold him up in the distorting mirror of *real-politik* as a Welsh Jean Marie Le Pen. But the politics of R.S. Thomas cuts across simple, modish poles of Left and Right in a way which is genuinely revolutionary. For unlike most who are free with their opinions of Wales, he has evolved a vision of the nation in which politics comprises a totality of experience that goes far beyond the limits we normally impose upon its meaning.

The essays in *Pe Medrwn yr Iaith* range over subjects that have occupied him for a long time: nuclear weapons, peace, nature, ornithology, the rural Welsh way of life, England and the English, industrial mass culture, the Church, *Cymraeg*. They cover, too, books he has read which he thinks are important: Dee Brown's *Bury My Heart at Wounded Knee*, Johnathan Schell's *The Fate of the Earth*, Fritjof Capra's *The Tao of Physics*; dealing respectively with the destruction of the American Indians, the implications for the Earth of nuclear war, the attempt by a physicist to reconcile Eastern mysticism with Western particle physics.

In the West 'We murder to dissect', obsessed with categories, divisions and subdivisions of the universe of which we are a part. But as R.S. Thomas suggests in 'Undod' all things are one. So in these essays, themes are not set out as discrete interests or concerns but are integrated in such a way that writing about one naturally draws out

[1] Ed. Tony Brown and Bedwyr Lewis Jones (Christopher Davies, 1988). Tony Brown's introduction was published in an English version in *The Powys Review*, 27 (1988).
[2] An English translation appeared in *Planet*, 70 (1988).

correspondences with others, and the reader is presented with a living body of thought.

It might be predicted that R.S. Thomas would see a parallel between the destruction of the plains Indians and their culture by American whites and the fate of the *Cymry*, while acknowledging the disparity in suffering. But a more significant example of his way of thinking is *'Adaryddiaeth—Beth Amdani?'* (Ornithology—What About It?). His concern for Welsh-language culture and his pleasure in bird-watching are well-known, but readers of *Barn* in 1967, where the article first appeared, are unlikely to have expected an essay with such a title to begin like this:

> *Y mae Cymru'n tyfu'n genedl gyfoes. Daeth ei deallusion i sylweddoli fod yn rhaid iddi groesawu a derbyn darganfyddiadau'r dydd, os ydyw am fyw. Daethant hefyd i weld y diffygion a'r bylchau yn ei thraddodiad.*

> Wales is becoming a contemporary nation. Her intellectuals came to realize that it was necessary to accept the discoveries of the day if she was to live. They also came to see the defects and gaps in her tradition.

From this starting point, the essay opens onto a discussion of the culture of the *Cymry*, contrasting a European Wales of the Middle Ages that absorbed influences directly from other cultures, with Wales as a little-regarded province of England which since the Act of Union has had such influences filtered through metropolitan English culture, *'gyda'r canlyniad mai'n hwyr iawn yr oeddynt yn dod, os dod o gwbl'* (with the consequence that they came late, if they came at all).

But a culture consists of its sciences as well as its arts, and though R.S. Thomas warns against things that savour too much of the English (*'sawru gormod o'r Sais'*), his own passion for ornithology causes him to recognize that the English were pioneers in the field from its inception in the nineteenth century. In science, he knows, there is no place for nationalism, *'ac eto trwy astudiaeth hir a manwl o natur fel yr ymddengys yn ei wlad ef y cyfrannodd llawer gwyddonydd at dwf ein gwybodaeth ohoni'* (yet though long and detailed study of nature as it manifests itself in his own country, many a scientist has contributed to the growth of our knowledge of it).

Which leads him back to Wales, a country with a varied bird population, situated on a major migration route, yet where the Welsh show hardly any interest in the subject. In fact, ornithology in Wales has been fostered by dedicated Englishmen and it is *'trist'*, sad, to think

5

'*mai Saeson oedd y cyntaf i godi arsyllfa ar Ynys Enlli, lle a fu'n enwog am ganrifoedd fel cyrchfan pererinion Cymraeg*' (that Englishmen were the first to establish an observatory on Ynys Enlli which was renowned for centuries as a resort of Welsh pilgrims).

Yet better the English than no one— '*gwell Saeson na neb*'.

Indifference to the natural world is evidence of the patchiness of Welsh culture, its incompleteness. In a rounded culture ornithology would have a definite place and would be accessible through that culture's language. (Denmark, for example, where I lived and watched birds for many years, has its own Ornithological Union, ornithologists with an international reputation, an authoritative two-volume *Danmarks Fugle* [Birds of Denmark].)

The lack of a Welsh ornithology, he argues, is an expression of our client status, where an imposed education system has taught us provinciality and how to turn our backs on natural history and that kind of nonsense ('*ffwlbri*') in favour of getting on in the world. As a result, Wales has produced two generations that have no interest in nature, who do not even know the Welsh names for birds, and who as a consequence no longer know how to live in rural Wales: '*Oblegid os ydych am fyw bywyd llawn yno, mae'n hanfodol i chi wybod cymaint ag sy'n bosibl amdani.*' (Because if you are to live a full life there, it is essential for you to know as much about it as possible.)

So an essay on ornithology becomes an exploration of the meaning of culture and a contribution to the revival of a full Welsh life. Small beginnings—the teaching of Welsh names for birds, for example—will help regain the world of nature so that it is seen through Welsh eyes.[3] For *Pe Medrwn yr Iaith* is insistent on one point: '*diwylliant yw iaith*', culture is language.

And that brings the argument around to Saunders Lewis and the vexed question of the 'English-speaking Welsh'.

It is significant that R. S. Thomas's ideas about Wales, and about politics in a nation like Wales, are rooted deeply in the early thinking of Saunders Lewis. In his lecture *Egwyddorion Cenedlaetholdeb* (Principles of Nationalism), given to the first Plaid Cymru summer school in 1926, Saunders Lewis made an important distinction between

---

[3] While this reflects the general situation in the mid 1960s, it has been pointed out to me that it fails to take into account the pioneering work of Ted Breeze Jones over the past forty years. More recently, of course, the situation has improved, thanks to societies like *Cymdeithas Edward Llwyd* which publishes *Y Naturiaethwr*, and to the existence of a growing number of Welsh nature books as well as the popular natural history magazine *Cynefin*.

nationalism as it developed from the sixteenth century—a tyranny of centralist states whose power depended on the suppression of the diverse languages and cultures that had existed during the feudal period of the Middle Ages; with a nationalism which is the struggle for and the expression of just such a language, such a culture.

Saunders Lewis warns against arguing for the rights of Wales on the basis of historical nationalist philosophy, *'Canys dadl faterol yw hi; ac mewn dadl faterol, y trechaf a dreisia.'* (For it is a materialistic argument; and in a materialistic argument, might is right.) He is explicit on this point: *'Rhaid i'n cenedlaetholdeb ni fod yn wahanol. Rhaid inni apelio nid at hawliau materol ond at egwyddorion ysbrydol.'* (Our nationalism must be different. We must appeal not to material rights but to spiritual principles.) For what is at stake is not the independence of Wales but its civilization and that, as Saunders Lewis saw so clearly, is dependent on language.

Central to his policy, therefore, is the Cymricization of Wales through a Welsh-medium education from primary school to university: *'Felly, fe etifedda pob plentyn yng Nghymru, pa iaith bynnag a fo iaith ei fam, y diwylliant Cymreig a'r iaith sy'n unig allwedd i'r diwylliant hwnnw.'* (Thus, every child in Wales, whatever his mother-tongue, will inherit Welsh culture and the language which is the only key to that culture.)

Defined in this way, politics is culture and culture language. Plaid Cymru should seek self-government for a Welsh-speaking Wales because without self-government *'ni ellir sicrhau'n derfynol gynnydd y diwylliant Cymraeg'* (we cannot definitely ensure the furtherance of Welsh culture). That is its sole purpose. Independence at any cost— an independent English-speaking Wales, for example—would be a retrograde step, a descent into 'the old materialistic nationalism'.

This leads Saunders Lewis into waters that have been considered murky since the 1930s. The distinctive quality of Welsh (*Cymraeg*) culture is its cultivation of poetry and music often under difficult circumstances. This is contrasted with the mass industrial culture of the English and the inroads of that culture in Wales wherever the English language becomes dominant:

> *Lle y bo'r Gymraeg yn fyw a chadarn, yno y ceir eisteddfodau lleol llewyrchus, cyfarfodydd llenyddol, dosbarthiadau darllen, ysgolion cân, a diddordeb gwiw mewn llên a cherdd. A pha le bynnag y nycho'r Gymraeg, a dyfod moes ac iaith y Saeson i'w lle hi, yno fe ddirywia'r pethau hyn, a cheir chwaraeon pêl droed a rasus a chlwbiau biliard a'r sinema, ac os bydd dosbarth o gwbl dan nawdd y colegau, mwy na thebyg mai dosbarth mewn economeg a fydd hwnnw.*

Where Welsh is alive and vigorous, there you will find flourishing local *eisteddfodau*, literary meetings, reading classes, singing schools and an admirable interest in literature and music. And wherever Welsh declines, and the English way of life and language replaces it, there these things degenerate, and one finds football matches, races, billiard clubs and the cinema, and if there is any class at all held under the aegis of the colleges, it will more than likely be a class in economics.

The essays in *Pe Medrwn yr Iaith* act as resonators by means of which Saunders Lewis's ideas are made plain to the next generation. There is a direct echo of 'Principles of Nationalism' in 'Arian a Swydd' (Money and Position) published in *Y Fflam* in 1946: *'Cyhyd ag y bo bwyd a diod, milgwn a sinemâu, ni waeth gan y mwyafrif o'n pobl pa lywodraeth sydd mewn bod.'* (As long as there is food and drink, greyhounds and cinemas, the majority of our people do not care what government is in power.)

In 'Abercuawg' (1976) he contrasts a visionary Wales which is very similar to Saunders Lewis's traditional Wales of the *Cymry* with one dominated by Western materialist civilization, overcrowded, homogenized, soul-less, dull. A year later in 'O'n Cwmpas' (Round About Us) he identifies the rallying cry of the Welsh as *'Bara o flaen harddwch!'* (Bread before beauty!) which is an excuse for the desertion and spoilation of the land.

'A ydwyf yn erbyn cynnydd?' (Am I against progress?) he asks in the same essay. *'Bydd digon yn dweud felly. Efallai fy mod i, i raddau.'* (There are plenty who say so. Perhaps I am to a degree.) A rhetorical hesitation perhaps, but made at a point where he knows his argument will seem weakest to the modern world. For underlying his thinking here as elsewhere is a suspicion of twentieth-century democracy which he inherited from Saunders Lewis and which the latter shared with such ideologues of the Right as T.S. Eliot, Wyndham Lewis and Ezra Pound.

'Gwir yw bod gan y Cymry enw da fel pobl ddemocrataidd, ond, yn fy marn i, y maent yn dangos y gwendidau i gyd sydd yn perthyn i ddemocratiaeth.' (It is true that the Welsh have a good reputation as a democratic people, but, in my opinion, they show all the weaknesses that belong to democracy.) These words are from 'Arian a Swydd'. Even in 1946 R.S. Thomas was making statements which challenge basic assumptions of this society.

It is possible to view the evident scorn for the mass culture of English industrial society, and the doubts about democracy, as a reactionary stance. It is easy then to dismiss R.S. Thomas and Saunders Lewis as political thinkers, rather than to re-evalute one's own position in the light of their criticisms. Even if they are wrong, important questions are being asked that need to be thought through by their liberal and left-wing opponents.

From the beginning Saunders Lewis believed that Welsh national-ist involvement in British politics was wrong. If Plaid Cymru contested parliamentary seats they should not send representatives to Westminster, for *'Tra fyddom fel yna yn rhan boliticaidd o Loegr ffolineb yw dadlau dros addysg Gymraeg i Gymru. Canys ystyr "rhan boliticaidd" yw "rhan gymdeithasol", sef rhan o wareiddiad Lloegr.'* (While we are thus a political part of England it is folly to argue for Welsh education for Wales. For 'political part' means 'social part', that is, part of English civilisation.) And that means part of the materialist mass culture that Saunders Lewis and R.S. Thomas after him see as being so debilit-ating.

At the end of his review of *Bury My Heart at Wounded Knee* R.S. Thomas urges *'Codwch chi, y Cymry'* (Rise up, you Welsh) to demand self-government in order to ensure that the future of Wales is consis-tent with its own distinctive traditions, *'cyn ei bod hi'n rhy hwyr'* (before it is too late).

But the call reflects the darker tones of Saunders Lewis's later think-ing as exemplified in his 1962 radio talk 'Tynged yr Iaith' (The Fate of the Language). There he sees his earlier optimism as misplaced. Even in 1926 the time had passed when Wales could be revived as *Cymru*. Now he believes that if the language is to be restored to Wales at all it must be by revolutionary means— *'Trwy ddulliau chwyldro yn unig y mae llwyddo.'* (Success is only possible through revolutionary methods.) By this he clearly means non-democratic, non-violent direct action of the kind taken up by *Cymdeithas yr Iaith Gymraeg.* And the reason for this is the old one: involvement in British politics, that is, English politics, means compromise in a situation where compromise is unacceptable because it will be on English terms. The history of the Liberal and Socialist parties in Wales is evidence enough of this.

Fourteen years after 'Tynged yr Iaith' R.S. Thomas takes up the same argument in 'Abercuawg'. There are those who believe *'mai'r unig ffordd i ddyfod ag Abercuawg i fod neu i'w hamddiffyn wedyn ydyw trwy beidio â rhwystro datblygiadau cyfoes, eithr ceisio eu troi at ddibenion da'* (that the only way to bring Abercuawg into existence, or to defend it subsequently, is by not interfering with contemporary developments, but rather seeking to channel them towards good ends). That is good thinking in terms of conventional parliamentary democracy. *'Ond nid trwy gyfaddawdu y cyrhaeddwn ni Abercuawg.'* (But it is not through compromise that we shall arrive at Abercuawg.)

R.S. Thomas isolates and challenges here one of the basic assumptions of Western mass democratic politics, with which Plaid Cymru has increasingly identified itself. That is, the conviction that in the world of *real-politik* the essence of policy is compromise. But in the world as it is in the late twentieth century, in almost every sphere, compromise offers too little too late. Wales, even as a shadow of Saunders Lewis's vision, cannot survive on a politics of compromise of the kind attempted recently by the leadership of Plaid Cymru. It involves too many concessions that appear to offer short-term solutions to the problems of a continuing Welsh identity, but which in reality abet the slide into British provincialism.

R.S. Thomas's thinking goes beyond the survival of Wales, however. All is one. The future of Wales as a cultural entity living through its language, *Cymraeg*, cannot be separated from the fate of the Earth itself. And here a strain of thought, anti-democratic in many of its assumptions, which in the 1920s and 1930s ran parallel with and could be confused with that of the right-wing ideologues, spirals off into a revolutionary course, though like all revolutionary thinking it will appear unacceptable because of some of its premises, to the liberal and left-wing *status quo*, which operates within a received frame of reference that is rarely questioned.

So while there are those who would agree with R.S. Thomas in objecting to nuclear arms and would support his stand against the destruction of nature, few would accept his identification of democracy in industrial mass society as one of the major causes of both.

It is a subject he explores in 'O'n Cwmpas'. The crisis we face now is the consequence of the developed nations thinking that the Earth's resources can never be exhausted. So industrialization ravages nature and we live with the results—massive conurbations, motorways, airports, pylons, acres and acres of land going under to development each year, in the name of progress, but really in the cause of greed and heedlessness. And how many Welsh people protest actively against the waste of the land, the destruction of beauty? *''Rwy'n hen gyfarwydd â'r waedd sydd yng Nghymru: Pobl sy'n cyfrif. Hidiwch befo natur a harddwch a phethau fel yna. Mae harddwch Cymru yn ei phobl!'* (I am more than familiar

10

with the cry in Wales: it is people who count. Never mind nature and beauty and things like that. The beauty of Wales is in its people!) But even if this is true, he argues, why can we not have both? He knows, however, that there is an attitude (*'agwedd'*) in Wales which treats those who love nature as if they were *de facto* against people.

And here again R.S. Thomas comes up against such entrenched assumptions about democratic society that to question them is to be labelled reactionary. But is it reactionary to suggest that there are too many people demanding too much of the Earth's resources, and that a place which depends on quietness for its beauty should be silently protected, and that people in their crowds should not be encouraged there?

Undemocratic, is the reply of those who want theme parks, country parks, walk-ways, pony trekking, mountain centres and holiday villages, picnic sites and easy access by car in the quiet places of Wales.

There is however an added complication. We demand these things as part of our freedom in a democratic society partly because we have become inured to the ugliness which encroaches on us daily. There is an indolence in mass society which makes people indifferent to the destruction of nature by authorities like the Forestry Commission and the CEGB. And there is a side to us which actively welcomes it:

> *Gwelsom lôn brydferth ac annwyl yn diflannu i roi lle i ffordd fawr gostus, a llongyfarch rhywun am ei fandaliaeth a wnaethom wrth ruthro yn ein blaenau yn ein cerbyd newydd sbon gan ddefnyddio gormod o betrol, maeddu'r awyr a rhoi bob math o fywyd arall mewn perygl.*

> We see a beautiful and beloved lane disappear to make way for an expensive main road, and we congratulate someone on his vandalism as we rush on in our brand new cars, using too much petrol and putting all kinds of other life forms in danger.

In the world as it is, everyone is complicit and no one escapes the consequences of that complicity. The nightmare we have created in the name of freedom reaches its height when we contemplate nuclear war. This is a preoccupation of the essays from the 1980s in *Pe Medrwn yr Iaith*. 'Yr Ateb i Ddifodiant' (The Answer to Annihilation), a commentary on Jonathan Schell's *The Fate of the Earth*, focuses on the hypocrisy of the argument for a nuclear deterrent. It is supposedly there to preserve freedom and democracy, yet, if used, all possibility of freedom and democracy would be obliterated for ever. Consequently people lead double lives, accommodating nuclear weapons that are

11

impossible to use while trying to live *'fel petae'r sefyllfa hunllefus yma heb fod'* (as if this nightmare situation did not exist).

Why do the majority accept this? Part of the answer, he suggests in 'Nadolig Niwcliar' (Nuclear Christmas) is in the propaganda machine of the Western democratic governments, which has been effective in persuading the public that nuclear weapons exist solely for peace and that anyone who says otherwise is 'a traitor or an extremist'. And this is backed up with self-contradictory lies: *'Mae'n bosibl ymladd rhyfel niwcliar a'i hennill.'* (It is possible to fight a nuclear war and win.) *'Mae'n bosibl amddiffyn eich hun rhag ymbelydredd fel y bydd digon o oroeswyr ar ôl y gyflafan i gynnal democratiaeth!'* (It is possible to protect yourself from radiation so that there will be enough survivors after the outrage to sustain democracy!)

Part of our problem is the philosophical assumptions that underly democracy and which are believed in such an unthinking way that anyone who questions them is an enemy of society. R.S. Thomas only touches on his doubts in these essays, implying that his audience will take them for granted, though he does indicate in 'Arian a Swydd' that in his opinion democracy has inherent flaws.

Some of these go back to its roots in late eighteenth-century radical thought: faith in the right-thinking of ordinary men and women, for example, which leads to the premise that a majority decision will somehow be the 'right' one, something which R.S. Thomas queries in 'Undod'. Another is the belief that democratic process and a free vote ensure changes in power that reflect the will of the people. It is a flaw because, as democracy has developed in the West, changes of government are usually cosmetic, real power lying with the permanent civil service, the police and the armed forces, the secret service, and above all with capital and industry, for industrial capitalism is historically the twin of mass democracy.

These things are, of course, known, though society's deep involvement in materialist culture ensures that they are not acted upon. But Wales like the other Celtic nations is more exposed to the flaws of the system because it is in every sense at the periphery of the centralist state's concern. In this century England has maintained its dominance because the Welsh have supported various forms of radical politics which whatever their colours have been deeply committed to British centralism.

Because of this, Saunders Lewis was right in 1926 to warn against Welsh nationalist involvement in English politics; just as he was right in 1962 to advocate 'revolutionary' methods as the only way to ensure the survival of Welsh-language culture. Such opinions are not popular because they imply that majority democracy is not necessarily right or just, and that a small dedicated group of men and women might work effectively against the will of the majority. That is why when R. S. Thomas called for a 'secret army' to defend the language, and when he expressed sympathy for *Meibion Glyndŵr*, he was bitterly criticized by those in Wales with a political interest in things as they are.

R.S. Thomas has a policy but it is one that operates outside the increasingly unacceptable confines of the democratic system. When elected governments are deeply complicit in the destruction of nature, when they justify nuclear arms in the name of humanity, and when a culture like that of the Welsh can be brought rapidly close to destruction by a system within which it can never achieve a power base, then it is hard to avoid non-democratic direct action, for democracy is foundering under the weight of its own contradictions.

In Wales, public support for *Meibion Glyndŵr* is presented as irresponsible by the authorities and the press. There are those in Wales who would disagree. And when one of the nation's finest poets, who began as a Christian pacifist, ends by advocating, no matter how circumspectly or metaphorically, revolution as the only hope for Welsh-language culture, it is at least an indicator of how desperate things have become.

Pe Medrwn yr Iaith is a testimony to this, as it is to the worth of that revolution if it can be achieved. The only shameful thing is that R.S. Thomas should be reviled for his ideas within his own nation. But as Saunders Lewis bitterly remarked: *'Yng Nghymru gellir maddau popeth ond bod o ddifri ynglŷn â'r iaith.'* (In Wales everything can be forgiven except being seriously concerned about the language.)

Never Forget Your Welsh

The title, *Welsh Airs*,[1] echoes those romanticized collections of folk ditties—'English Airs', 'Scottish Airs'—that were tidied up and set to piano accompaniment for use in lower middle class parlours of the last century. It is, of course, sardonic, for *Welsh Airs* is a selection of R.S. Thomas's verse attacks on the Welsh that pepper his work from *The Stones of the Field* (1946) to *Not That He Brought Flowers* (1968). These are supplemented by fourteen more recent and previously uncollected poems on the same theme. In a sense, therefore, this is a 'Selected Poems' which follows the iniquitous habit of contemporary publishers who tack on a dozen or so poems to a 'Selected' to draw in those readers who already have the original collections.

In another sense it is quite different. For what has always been a thread in the poetry is now picked out and presented as a major theme. The new poems, and the presence of early ones such as 'Border Blues' which are extremely hard to come at elsewhere, make *Welsh Airs*, therefore, a new collection—and coming at this point in his poetic career, a testament, a witness, to the way the Welsh, as he sees it, have betrayed themselves as a people.

One of R.S. Thomas's early mentors was Saunders Lewis. There are two poems about him here, 'The Patriot' and the previously un-collected 'Saunders Lewis'. Each emphasises the close relation between poetry, the Welsh language and patriotism in Saunders Lewis's life. He is for R.S. Thomas the exemplary Welsh artist, whose art will not let the people rest, for

> when he wrote
> Drawing ink from his own veins'
> Blood and iron, the sentences
> Opened again the concealed wounds
> Of history in the comfortable flesh.
> ('The Patriot')

In 'Saunders Lewis' R.S. Thomas goes further. It is an irregular sonnet, the octave of which reads:

> And he dared them;
> Dared them to grow old and bitter

[1] R. S. Thomas, *Welsh Airs* (Poetry Wales Press, 1987).

As he. He kept his pen clean
By burying it in their fat
Flesh. He was ascetic and Wales
His diet. He lived off the harsh fare
Of her troubles, worn yet heady
At moments with the poets' wine.

These lines reveal the deep correspondence of feeling R.S. Thomas has with Saunders Lewis, now, in old age. He could lean back as the acknowledged elder statesman of Welsh literature (in English). Instead, he has accepted that dare, grown old and bitter, with a bitterness born out of seeing the betrayal of the language by the Welsh— R.S. Thomas always reserves his fiercest comments for his own, despite the harsh things he has to say about the English. You can be conquered from without; you can only be defeated from within.

But there is a bitterness which is also a stubbornness, an insistence that when the Welsh as a people seem to be coming to an end, there should still be witnesses. It is, however, easier to temporize, to be a trimmer, to persuade ourselves that we are not sliding with the inevitability of continental drift into English provincialism, and that the death of the Welsh language does not mean the death of Welsh consciousness and culture. 'Saunders Lewis' ends:

Small as he was
He towered, the trigger of his mind
Cocked, ready to let fly with his scorn.

R.S. Thomas has not only taken up the dare to grow old and bitter, he has also taken on Saunders Lewis's mantle as consciousness of a people that would sooner forget.

A recurring theme in *Welsh Airs* is of Wales as a carcass, the body politic of the nation quite dead, but picked over by the Welsh for anything saleable and settled on by flies from England 'befouling our winding-sheet/with their droppings' ('Toasts'). A carcass, however, cannot feel the sting of the buck-shot of these poems, and the English, settlers and others, are unlikely to understand what the fuss is about. 'What shall I say,' he asks in 'Toast'

to a people to whom provincialism
is a reasonable asking price
for survival?

The answer?

15

                I salute your
        astuteness and drink to your future
        from a wine-glass brimming with acid rain.

The multiple meanings of 'acid' in that last image have an important bearing on the meaning of this book. For behind the scorn for the Welsh which R.S. Thomas is more than willing to let fly, is knowledge of a Wales which existed, at certain times, in certain places, and which has existed for R.S. Thomas in moments which have become touchstones for his life and art, and which are the justification of the scorn.

Most people are incapable of sustaining intense negative emotion over many years, it wears them out, destroys their creativity if they are artists. Yet this has not happened to R.S. Thomas whose art has sustained its quality, reaching out since *H'm* into deeper and other channels. There are two reasons, at least, for this. One was the move to Aberdaron on Pen Llŷn where, he writes in *Neb*, he felt he had come home—to a place where he could live out his life naturally through the medium of Welsh. The other, equally evident in *Neb* and the poetry, is the sustaining power of nature, not only in the constant surprises of the beauty of rural Wales, but in the deeper sense of nature as an intimation of the divine, the sense Wordsworth had that moonlit night on Snowdon of nature as 'the emblem of a mind/That feeds upon infinity'.

But even in the 1800s, Wordsworth was aware that the potential for such experience was in danger. Side by side with the celebration of nature is the knowledge of how social change was destroying the economic base of the 'Statesmen', the independent hill farmers and shepherds of his childhood Westmoreland. *Michael* ends with the family farm sold-off to a stranger, the farm itself ploughed under, and Michael's son, Luke, lost in the industrial city.

R. S. Thomas's haven on Pen Llŷn is being lost in the same way. House after house is for sale, the peace of the natural world is shattered by low-flying fighters, violated by tourists, the countryside built over for the holiday industry, planted over by the Forestry Commission. All this, and the Welsh not stubbornly resisting like Michael, but conniving at nature's and their own destruction.

That is why the bitterness remains and deepens; and why it flashes out in the new poems in this book, where he returns to the attack. For there is no escape. The acid toast, with acid rain in the wine glass, is to a people who cannot see that their identity as a people is bound up with

16

the language, and the language with the land. Like Wordsworth, he sees the wilder, bleaker aspects of nature as essential to the spirit, and also essential to Welshness. Just as a certain kind of poverty is: not the poverty of abject want in an unjust economic system, but the voluntary poverty known as patient poverty, an inner resistance to the blandishments of the world, which medieval ascetics practised.

But how many of us are willing to put up with that? The temptations are too great:

> Four centuries now
> We have been leaving
> The hills and the high moors
> For the jewelled pavements
> Easing our veins of their dark peat
> By slow transfusions.
>
> ('Expatriates')

In the land of Barratt houses and consumer durables, Welsh as a language of the spirit would have died in any case, just as surely as the English which is replacing it, and as English settlers replace us in the countryside:

> All this beauty,
> and all the pain
> of beholding it emptied
> of a people who were not worthy of it.
>
> ('Deprivation')

And as the process of decline continues, what was a living culture becomes a relic in the hands of scholars, annotators, translators, the poetry explained in footnotes, once-famous men and women who lived in a people's imagination reduced to 'asterisks and numbers'— 'Branwen (Refer Below)' ('Dead Worthies').

Welsh Airs ends with 'Fugue for Ann Griffiths', R.S. Thomas's longest poem for some time. It may seem a strange, inappropriate ending, at odds with the acerbic poems that form the bulk of this collection. But its themes are the familiar ones: how in Wales poetry, spiritual replenishment, lives led close to nature, are the inseparable determinants of Welsh culture. Or were in Ann's time, living as she did in 'A nineteenth century/calm' which is defined as

> . . . a countryside
> not fenced in
> by cables and pylons,

but open to thought to blow in
    from as near as may be
to the truth.

The calm is gone, and with it openness to thought of the kind possessed by Ann Griffiths; for what we want now is distraction from thought which might lead us to a truth we do not want to know.

There is a sense in this poem of R.S. Thomas, too, having known something of what Ann knew, but only at great cost in a world that no longer values such knowledge. Many of the earlier poems in the book are public lambastings of the Welsh for failure of nerve, for servility. The 'Fugue' stands back from all this, looks—like some of his poems on nineteenth-century French paintings—from our time to a time when a road was 'not for getting people/anywhere, at least/not at speed' ('Monet: The Bas-Bréau Road').

In the 'Fugue' the question of the people, the carcass of its body politic, is let fall, is over. The poem turns on an individual's readiness to come at inner truth in a Wales that has all but ceased to exist, buried under the detritus of our civilization. What can we learn now from Ann's religious letters, her hymns, her life? The answer is the mystic's paradox: all our roads are going nowhere; you can only find direction by standing still:

So with wings pinned
and fuel rationed,
let us put on speed
to remain still
through the dark hours
in which prayer gathers
on the brow like dew,
where at dawn the footprints
of one who invisibly
but so close passed
discover a direction.

The book ends, then, on a note of resolution, of possibility for the individual. But not for the nation. Behind this hesitant hope lies poem after poem on how we have sold ourselves out and sold ourselves short. Maelgwyn, sixth-century King of Gwynedd, 'kept his power/By intelligence', while

    we lose
Ours for lack of it,
Holding our caps out

18

Beside a framed view
We never painted, counting
The few casual cowries
With which we are fobbed off.

          ('Traeth Maelgwyn')

Holding out caps suggests the servility of the street beggar, while 'cowries' echoes tourist tales of how quaint or cheap things are in Melanesia or Morocco—the fine intrusion of 'casual' intimating at the same time the Westerner's inner disdain for those who sell themselves, or beg.

But there is another kind of selling, dealt with only obliquely, if at all, in this book: the hard sell in recent years of a literature which is English in language, but—so the spiel goes—entirely Welsh in subject-matter and resonance. Nowadays you can be just as Welsh in English: no need to learn the old language. Being Welsh is an ambience, is somehow in the air; though it helps if you refer to Welsh subjects and places to clue the reader in. This is, of course, a descent into provincialism. A Welsh-language writer can treat of any subject, and his or her work is Welsh by virtue of its medium, *Cymraeg*. For a Danish writer it is the same: there is no constraint on subject-matter because the *national* identifier is inherent in the language. An 'Anglo-Welsh' writer, by contrast, has to keep pointing up the fact, for the reader and himself, that he is 'Welsh' by limiting his subject-matter to what might be termed the agreed 'Matter of Wales'. Outside that, what is to distinguish an 'Anglo-Welsh' from an English writer? The answer, though most Welsh authors writing in English do not like it, and will go on denying it, is—nothing. Unless, that is, you do as R.S. Thomas has done, and align yourself with the magnetic field of Welsh-language culture. So your English words come alive as Welsh by a form of symbiosis. By its nature, however, this must be a personal achievement, dependent on the existence of the Welsh language and on the individual writer's affirmation of its significance. It is a fragile relationship which only a great writer could achieve. For that reason alone it is unlikely to lead to a tradition.

Across the Grain

Neb[1] is R.S. Thomas's autobiography, though perhaps it would be more accurate to say apologia, for rather than a minutely detailed account of his life it offers an explanation of his conduct and opinions. It is an apologia, however, intended for a particular audience, the only one I suspect whose opinion he would now consider important—the *Cymry Cymraeg*. For this reason it is written in Welsh and documents the life-long attempt of a man to turn himself into a Welshman, that is, one whose life is lived through the medium of the Welsh language.

The metamorphosis might have been complete, were it not for the fact that R.S. Thomas is a poet. No one that I know has succeeded in writing great poetry in anything other than his first language, and R.S. Thomas is aware of this to a high degree. It is one of the ironies of his life that his first language was English, the language of a nation he hates, deeply and corrosively, for what it has done to Wales. But precisely because it is his first language, it is the only one in which he can write poetry, and because a poet must know what has been achieved in the language he uses if he is to write well, R.S. Thomas is as deeply indebted to poets like Wordsworth and Coleridge, whose ideas are frequent touchstones in this book, as he is to the Welsh poetic tradition.

There is further irony in his choice of a ministry in the Church in Wales, for even if it is disestablished, it is still the Church *in* Wales, not *of* Wales; the Church that symbolizes English ascendancy, the product of a typically English Reformation compromise with Catholicism. The culture of the Welsh Wales he identifies with is rooted in Nonconformity, but though he admires Nonconformists in many ways, not least for their support of the language, R.S. Thomas has never been able to sympathize with Nonconformity itself: '. . . he was never comfortable in chapel. There was a lack of taste, a lack of atmosphere. He knew also of the weakness of chapel organization. Things like this made it impossible for him to worship effectively in a chapel, or to receive Communion there.' He also found Nonconformist familiarity with God distasteful, and for these reasons had grave reservations about reunification.

[1] Edited by Gwenno Hywyn, *Cyfres y Cewri* 6 (Gwasg Gwynedd, 1985).

Yet relations with the Church in Wales were far from happy. Increasingly, his own commitment to Welsh nationalism was paralleled by the Church's abandonment of precisely those traditions which made R.S. Thomas Anglican rather than Nonconformist: the new translation of the Bible was anathema to him, for example, and to the end of his ministry he held to the Authorized Version and the 1662 Book of Common Prayer. Then there were running battles with the Church authorities over issues such as bilingual church registers. The Registrar General in London had ruled that the first entry must be in English, and that Welsh might be omitted at the discretion of the minister. When R.S. Thomas made numerous protests at the injustice of this, he was finally silenced by the Rural Dean who told him that Aberdaron was the only parish to keep bilingual records anyway.

R.S. Thomas writes that he never found any conflict of interest between his vocations as priest and poet, but there was clearly a profound one between himself as a Welshman and the Anglican Church he served. Had he been a Nonconformist minister there would have been no tension over nation and language, yet as a Church in Wales priest in Eglwys-fach, he found himself ministering to a parish dominated by the English middle class, including a heavy sprinkling of retired army officers, about whom he has harsh things to say. At Aberdaron he had to stand in the church porch and endure an Englishwoman visitor turn and say, 'I'm sorry we didn't pray for the Queen!' And of course R.S. Thomas could only think of the appropriate reply afterwards: 'Woman, be thankful you had a service at all in your foreign language.'

The problem of language is a nagging theme throughout *Neb*. R.S. Thomas has refined English in powerful ways that only a great poet can, but to achieve this in the very language that is destroying Welsh, the language of his nation and spirit, is an irony almost too hard to bear. When he moved to Aberdaron, a place where he speaks Welsh as a matter of course each day, he felt he had arrived at a true spiritual home, and 'Because of this, he looked at the language on the lips of visitors [i.e. tourists]. Very quietly, he cursed their language.' This is one of the deepest rifts in a man divided against himself in complex ways. English is projected outwards here as 'their' language, yet it is his language too, the one which, through his profession of poetry, he has used to express his sensibility. Because of this, such hatred of English is a form of self hatred.

21

When you have established a reputation as one of the best poets of your time, it may seem odd, even perverse, to call your autobiography *Neb* (Any one; No one). But the problem of identity it poses has absorbed R.S. Thomas's attention from the beginning. When he was a young minister at Manafon, he had been repelled by the apparent vacancy of mind, the spiritual nullity of the hill farmers, induced by their hard lives on the land. To him, then, it was almost as if they had no identity.

At Eglwys-fach he was sickened by the opposite: the pretensions of his middle-class English parishioners that they were *somebody*, all 'playing some rôle, consciously or unconsciously, competing with each other to seem a person of substance who could look back on a successful career'. These people were better educated and more artic-ulate than the Manafon farmers had been, yet their shallow preten-sions raised the question 'to what degree they were conscious at all?' And the more disturbing corollary: 'Can a man face life if he feels he is no one?'

The problem of identity, or the lack of it, is one most of us push to the back of the mind, unless we are forced to confront it through some crisis. It is, however, a problem R.S. Thomas has been led to confront through his vocation as a poet, for 'The creative artist has to be pain-fully honest with himself. He has to look as objectively as possible on his creations. What is the purpose in pretending that a poem is good, if it is not?' It is perhaps this habit of the scrutiny of his work that explains R.S. Thomas's unusual use of the third person singular in *Neb*. Not 'I' but 'he', 'R.S.', did this, thought that—the individual life distanced, appraised as far as possible with a dispassionate eye. The self-knowledge that may emerge from such a process can be frightening, and no wonder that most of us avoid it if we can.

Disturbing, too, is the contemplation of our lifespan as individual human beings in the context of geological time. On Pen Llŷn, R. S. Thomas encountered the Pre-Cambrian rocks of Braich-y-pwll, and 'realized he was in contact with something which had been there for a thousand million years. It made him dizzy. Such a time scale raised all kinds of questions and problems. On seeing his shadow fall on such ancient rocks, he was obliged to question himself in a different context, and ask the same old question as before: "Who am I?" And the answer came back more emphatic than ever: "No one".'

The shadow of man has been a potent symbol in R.S. Thomas's poetry, from the shadow of the hill farmer forming its question mark on the field, to his own falling on the rock on Pen Llŷn. It is one of the sources for his pessimism. Yet to leave things there would be to accept a Larkinesque nihilism, and this has never been R.S. Thomas's position. As epigraph to *Neb* he quotes a line from a poem by Paul Claudel— *'Et de ce néant indestructible, qui est moi'*. It is a paradox that cannot properly be paraphrased, but it is illumined in some of R. S. Thomas's finest poems, and contains a tension of contradictory feelings which is central to *Neb*. After asking at Braich-y-pwll 'Who am I?' and receiving again the answer 'No one', he continues: 'But no one with a halo of light about his head,' recalling a verse of Pindar: 'Man is a dream about shadow. But when some splendour falls on him from god, glory comes to him and his life is sweet.'

For R.S. Thomas such moments are bound up with nature. Having divested himself of all pretensions to self at Braich-y-Pwll, he tells how the natural world of the peninsula sometimes seemed so intense an experience that 'he thought he had been there forever, a part of the unbroken chain of being'. The experience recalls those 'spots of time' in Wordsworth's *The Prelude*, when the intense perception of the actuality of things is suspended in a moment which is entirely within time yet seemingly timeless, during which the self is annihilated.

This is a kind of nature mysticism which places R.S. Thomas firmly in the Romantic tradition that has meant so much to him as a writer, as does his tendency to see nature in symbolic as well as literal terms. In *Neb* he describes watching the sun emerge over the sea after bad weather, as sky and sea in turn become charged with blue. He comments: 'This is a symbol of a burden lifted from the spirit after a period of despair.' There are many such moments in *Neb*, as there are in the poems. Nature for R.S. Thomas is Wordsworthian: a world which intermingles with the consciousness of man on one level, and provides intimations of the transcendental on the other.

Such a view celebrates a living penetrative world, where the beholder half creates what he sees, as in this perception of Pen Llŷn on a fine day as 'a long bough suspended between sea and sky'. The Earth is not objective, 'out there', but subjective, inextricably bound up with our perception of it. In this Coleridgean view of perception, the quality of our seeing half determines the world we live in, making it more—or less—a habitable place for humankind.

R.S. Thomas's view of nature is far from sentimental, however. His observation of the harsh lives of the farmers at Manafon was enough to dispel any illusion of the countryside as rural idyll. He is aware, too, of the dark side, from a human perspective, of the natural world. The sea features prominently in *Neb* as an exhilarating force central to his imagination. But he knows it both as a window and a mirror. As a mirror it reflects the beauty of nature; as a window it reveals 'a perpetual war, one creature devouring another without pity and without end'. This is a post-Darwinian view that R.S. Thomas shares with Ted Hughes. For each it darkens and deepens his understanding of nature without, however, destroying his essential Romantic relation to it.

Moreover, these contraries find a reflection within R.S. Thomas himself. As a pacifist he could never openly advocate violence, even in the cause of Wales, though 'The worst of it is that the Englishman respects violence, just as he respects anyone who resists him.' Yet at Manafon he had had to come to terms with the cruelty of farmers toward their animals, people for whom killing was, and had to be, a way of life. And as a birdwatcher he cannot help a sense of exhilaration at the violence of raptors, whose beauty is so great. 'Anyone who saw a peregrine falcon descend like lightning on its prey would be sure to feel a thrill, which would make him humble. Here are the masters of the natural world.'

For R.S. Thomas, as for Ted Hughes, the horror inherent in life on Earth questions the nature of God. Here they part company, though, for Hughes rejects Christianity for a species of Lawrentian paganism, while R.S. Thomas falls back on Christian doubt. With a finite understanding in a world of contraries, 'How do you know?' he asks, echoing Blake.

Yet if the endless cycle of pitiless killings in nature questions the existence of a God of Love, nature also is the paradoxical foundation of R.S. Thomas's faith, and here again he is close to Wordsworth. He notes that Christianity itself is deeply rooted in the natural world, and cites Christ's parables as example. For the poet, too, nature provides constant analogies for the Christian life, confirming him in his belief. 'Going into the peace and beauty of a moor was like going into a church more beautiful than any he had ever seen. And gazing at the morning dew in the sun was like listening to the choir of heaven singing to the glory of God.'

Commenting on these experiences, R.S. Thomas adds, 'He wondered if he could go on believing in an industrial town.' It is a question he voices several times in *Neb*, for the beauty of nature is integral to his understanding of the divine. 'According to Thomas

Aquinas, God reveals himself in such a way that his creatures can accept him. If he did this to R.S., he chose to do it through the means of the natural world.'

But in his lifetime, R.S. Thomas has seen the natural world whittled away by human use, the peace of Pen Llŷn disrupted by jet fighters and in summer by tourists. In a memorable passage, he asks the reader to imagine

> a man fifty years ago getting off a train at a small station deep in the Welsh countryside at night. The first thing that would come to his ears out of the darkness would be the sound of water descending from above. And on looking in the right direction, he would see the black shadow of the mountain between himself and the sky, and he would realize that he was not in England. That has disappeared forever. Today Wales is a land of pylons and wires, a land of television and police transmitter masts, a land of new roads crowded with strangers rushing to the sea, a place where [Forestry Commission] woods and caravan parks are busily swallowing up what open land is left. In the face of this, R.S. knew well why he had turned more and more to interest himself in birds.

And further and further from the mass of modern humanity.

I find his position hard to quarrel with, yet it is strange to find it in a priest. From the beginning of his ministry, R.S. Thomas seems to have had a low opinion of his parishioners. When he moved to Eglwys-fach he was relieved to have left behind the 'coarseness' of Manafon. But in his new parish, behind the veil of middle-class courtesy, the vicar 'learned about the old frailties of mankind, such as snobbery, envy and avarice'. No doubt a clergyman sees more than most of human pettiness and viciousness. What is surprising in *Neb* is the apparent absence of charity, which, one would think, must have made his vocation as a priest almost unendurable at times. God figures largely in the autobiography, as he does in the poems; so does the problem of faith. But there is little mention of Christ, the mediator of God's *caritas* to fallen humanity.

The truth is that R. S. Thomas is not much interested in the generality of human beings, and the austere, exacting standards he set for himself make him more ready to condemn that forgive, when he turns his attention to others. But one of the outstanding qualities of *Neb* is its scrupulous honesty in areas where many another would prefer to deflect the reader's attention elsewhere. 'Human kind/ cannot bear very much reality,' wrote Eliot; 'Truth Kills Everybody',

25

Hughes entitles one of his poems. Mostly we do not like to be told the truth:

> As his life begins to come to an end, does R.S. have any message, and advice to give? None. He did not get enough experience of human life to preach to anyone. To him, people tend to live in his imagination, instead of being part of his personal experience. As he was not a novelist, he had no need to follow people closely in order to study them in detail to make them living characters in a book. His opinion of people is that some are good and some are evil, with a large group, neither good nor evil, in the middle, which goes on its uninteresting way each day.

His most intense experiences, to judge from *Neb* and the poems, have been connected with nature, not man; nature as the mediator of a God whose grace, for R.S. Thomas, is present there in unexpected moments:

> I walked on
> Simple and poor, while the air crumbled
> And broke on me generously as bread.
> ('The Moor')

But this God is necessarily remote, manifesting himself through a nature which is non human. Such moments are a gift of grace but not an expression of *caritas*, which is mediated to humanity through Christ the Son. No wonder, in Christian tradition, Christ figures so prominently, for he can forgive what the poet in the image of his silent God can not.

In his Eisteddfod Genedlaethol lecture, *Abercuawg*, R.S. Thomas notes the ability of words to influence a man's life even more powerfully than facts. 'And one example of this strange power words have is myth—man's capacity to create figures and symbols which convey the truth to him in a more direct manner than could plain colourless facts.' This is the faculty of imagination in the Coleridgean sense, which enabled Coleridge as poet 'to fashion things which came closer to the truth than did the common things of life'.

R.S. Thomas has this faculty to a high degree. In the substantial body of his work, he has used it to create the possibility of faith—though a difficult, austere faith—in an age which seems to preclude belief for most. He has also imagined Wales for the English-speaking Welsh (and perhaps for some of the *Cymry Cymraeg*) more powerfully than any of his contemporaries.

It is symbolized by 'Abercuawg', the place where the cuckoos sing, but which exists only in the search for it—for to find it would be to find dust and disillusion. 'We are searching therefore, within time, for something which is above time, and yet, which is ever on the verge of being.' 'Where is Abercuawg?' is a question that echoes through a life-time's poems, just as it impelled the life itself from Maelor *Saesneg* to Manafon and from Eglwys-fach to Aberdaron. He comes close to it in those 'spots of time' that are also intimations of God's existence, and closest perhaps on Pen Llŷn.

The idea of a Wales, rural, Welsh-speaking, Christian, is a fundamental, generative idea for R.S. Thomas. It has provided some of his profoundest moments of illumination, and has been the cause of a bitterness that pervades *Neb*. For to look on the destruction of the Welsh countryside and the ebbing away of the Welsh language, is to question whether Abercuawg was ever more than a delusive dream. R.S. Thomas's *Cymru* is not a fashionable Wales for the majority. It is too austere, it demands too much of the Welsh in an age which is utilitarian and materialist. His vision, as *Neb* makes clear, is Romantic in the most positive sense. Wordsworth and Coleridge, too, cut across the grain of their times. The world went on in its commitment to 'progress'. But the great poems of the Romantic period came out of their insistence on values other than getting and spending. R.S. Thomas's poems, too, come out of the stubborn belief that the life we are bent on leading is against nature (including the deepest levels of human nature), and is wrong.

The Janus County

Since my childhood at least, a sign outside the town hall has proclaimed 'Abergavenny, Gateway to Wales'. I used to wonder about it: you pass through a gateway going to or coming from somewhere. A gateway is not a place. Yet my life seems to have been spent in this imaginary gateway's shadow, part of me looking across the hills deeper into Wales, part, Janus-like, over the rolling farmland into England. It is an intuition many people have in north-east Gwent and explains the frequent defensive bristle when someone irritably asserts or denies being Welsh—or English. Rural Gwent, two-thirds of the county, seems at times consigned by the Welsh to limbo, given over to the English who until the advent of tourism twenty years ago had never heard of it.

My first experience of a kind of culture-shock was when I went to university in Birmingham at nineteen. As the train approached Snow Hill Station, smoke-blackened walls closed in above, and I had a sinking feeling that I always associate now with cities. Day trips to Cardiff and a holiday in London had not prepared me for living in the endless drabness of a Victorian industrial city. Nor was I prepared for the university where all the teachers and nearly all the students were English and had an easy, unselfconscious acceptance of who and what they were. I felt awkwardly different; but if not English, then what?

Uncertain identity now seems to me part of living in Gwent, but my first conscious experience of it left me confused. The problem was compounded by the Jugoslav family with whom I lodged for more than three years. They introduced me to the large community of Serbian exiles in Birmingham: men and women mostly from rural backgrounds, caught up in the Second World War, watching their children adopt city ways and English mass culture, while they preserved with a fierce determination a Serbian culture of dance and song, and religion. Uprooted from place, and centred on language, it preserved for them a sense of identity. I enjoyed the feast days, the saints' festivals, the ring dances and songs; but here was another world intruding questions into mine. These people were deracinated but retained a culture of a kind that did not exist where I came from, and one which I could never be a part of. I seem to have spent my student years in a permanent state of irritability, at odds with myself and my surroundings without knowing why.

I later moved to Denmark where I lived for thirteen years, and that made me think about Gwent and Wales from yet another perspective. On occasions I found myself in situations where I spoke Danish almost exclusively for several days on end, and it led me to realize how profoundly the language you speak defines the person you are. It was not merely that now and again there was a concept for which I could find no word in Danish and vice versa, but that the rhythm, syntax and intonation of a language, as well as the layers of accumulated meaning inherent in words, tilt what you have to say off balance. To think and feel in another language is to inhabit a seemingly familiar world, yet where all the names are different on the maps. I began to realize how *other* must be the experience of a Welsh-speaking from an English-speaking Welshman, and it was in Copenhagen that I began to learn Welsh.

This again gave my Gwent upbringing a new dimension. Like most people in rural Gwent, I had grown up largely ignorant of the meaning of the Welsh names for rivers, hills, farms, villages and towns that surrounded me, mispronouncing them in a way which has become habitual in the area. Understanding what the names meant released me into a new relationship with the landscape. The Viking explorers of the Atlantic isles and Greenland took care to name every prominent point along the coast where they landed; the naming in a sense reinvented the landscape, claimed it as human and habitable. In a similar way, learning Welsh, however inadequately, gave me a new and unexpected relation to the landscape, and made me realize how alienating it is to live out your life in ignorance of the meaning of names you use every day. Whether only subconsciously, many people in Gwent must feel this, and it may help explain the unease, the irrational hostility to Welsh that explodes there so readily.

Yet English? Travel to Herefordshire, Gloucestershire or Avon, and the accents, the towns, the farms, alert you to a world that is subtly different. The Usk valley, narrowing into Powys, has greater affinities with rural mid Wales than England. There are the same farmhouses and outbuildings built of mountain stone and roofed in slate, the same pastoral economy, and behind the scarp slopes of the Black Mountains, the same precarious hill farms. Even an Anglicized town like Abergavenny fits more easily into a Welsh than an English context: from Roman garrison to Norman stronghold, through Tudor administrative centre to Royalist outpost, its history has been shaped by the need of the English to control the Welsh hinterland.

The rural north-east of the county is also experiencing the break-down of its settled communities due to the same complex of depopulation through lack of work and second home ownership, which forces house prices beyond the means of many locals, creating in some areas the illusion of ghost-hamlets throughout the week, until the weekend-cottagers return to soak-up the local colour which they themselves are helping to destroy. Second-home burnings have only taken place in the Welsh-speaking heartlands where the pressure on the language makes the issue at once clearer and more urgent, yet in the Black Mountains, too, tourism and the neo-landed gentry from the Midlands and Bristol and London are undermining a rural culture which if not Welsh was certainly not English.

It is, of course, the language and the proximity of the border which gives so much of rural Gwent its equivocal status. On most marches, language decides the issue: if you live on the German side of the Dano-German frontier, in Slesvig, you will be a German national; but if you happen to be born into one of the Danish-speaking communities there, you will feel yourself a Dane. In Gwent, language blurs the sense of identity—English-speaking, yet living in a county steeped in Welsh history and where the landscape has been given its human countenance in Welsh, how could it be otherwise? Had my paternal grandfather emigrated to Denmark a hundred years ago, his descendants would have been Danish. Instead he went to Monmouthshire, and we live still in the shadow of the gateway.

It would be wrong, though, merely to dismiss rural Gwent as a border area lost to Wales, for what has happened there is happening now in other counties that are far more deeply rooted in Welshness. When the Welsh language retreated north-west into Powys in the middle of the last century, it was the turning point in a long process of attrition, the result of which has been a period of uncertain identity, followed recently by rapid Anglicization. Some believe we can create a sense of Welsh nationhood through the medium of English like the Scots and the Irish. But this fails to take into account the different paths those nations took to the English language, as it fails to ask how Anglicized Ireland, perhaps, is now compared to the Gaelic-speaking nation it superseded. Not least important is the fact that English became the dominant language late in the history of Wales and has not developed even into a distinctive dialect. In any discussion of Welshness and the language, rural Gwent is an important example and a warning.

The Naming of Places

Recently I found myself ticking off the names of houses on a route I walk regularly: Tanglewood, Plas Newydd, Charnwood, Rapallo; three times a week one way, and three times back. Gradually the names fixed themselves in my mind and I began to wonder about them. Here is a more extensive list:

> Tanglewood, Plas Newydd, Charnwood, Westbrook, Chetwynd, Eardisland, Lea Bailey, Fell Side, Lea Croft, Lyncroft, Grantham, Noddfa, Setauket, Homeleigh, Waterloo Cottage, Willow Croft, Arosfa, Cresta, Cressbrook.

The list is a rag-bag, typical of the style and period of the houses and the social position of the owners: most were built randomly over the years since the 1920s in a part of Abergavenny which is lower middle to middle class. It is an extraordinary muddle of names, and reveals something of the original occupants' dreams and aspirations.

A surprising number have rural associations: Lea Croft, Lyncroft, Willow Croft, Homeleigh (with a pun on 'homely'?), Fell Side, Cress Brook, Westbrook, Charnwood. But 'croft' is not a word used for smallholdings in the Welsh border country, and these are town houses, not one-storey dwellings of the rural poor. A 'lea' is 'a tract of open ground, especially grass land' according to *The Concise Oxford Dictionary*, and its use is 'poetic', which in dictionary terms means absolute, not in common use. The only open tract of land nearby is the park, Bailey Park, which is referred to in Lea Bailey, the one house name on the list with any relevance to its surroundings. For at Willow Croft there are no willows; Homeleigh is not an open tract of land nearest the farm; Fell Side is in a flat, suburban street; there is no stream on the property at Westbrook or Cressbrook; and the latter, of course, has no cress, nor Charnwood a wood.

It is interesting to turn from the houses in the town to the farms in the surrounding hill country. Here is a representative list of their names, with literal translations where necessary:

> Glaswellt-teg (Fair Green Grass), Pen-twyn (Top of the Pitch), Maes-y-garth (Hill Enclosure), Little Pool Farm, Pen-y-Graig (Head of the Rock), Cwm-cegyr (Hemlock Cwm), Little Mill, Hafod Illtyd (Illtyd's Summer Dwelling), Pen-y-ffos-goch (Head of

the Red Dike), Fox's Bark, Gelli-lwyd (Grey Wood), Wern-ddu (Black Marsh), Hill Barn, Pant-y-tyle (Hill Vale), Ty'r Pwll Farm (Pool House Farm), Pen Rhos (Top of the Moor), Werngochlyn (Red Marsh Lake).

The Welsh language retreated from the hill farms of the Black Mountains in the middle of the nineteenth century, so that these names mostly represent a far older naming practice, coming out of an agricultural community. One striking feature of the list is the literally down to earth quality of the names. A farm is identified by its proximity to a salient feature of the landscape: Pen-twyn, Pen-y-ffos-goch, Wern-ddu; or by its location in a broader tract of land: Cwm-cegyr, Pant-y-tyle. Others indicate a notable feature of the land itself: Glaswellt-teg, Maes-y-garth; or identify a property either by the name of the owner, or, just possibly here, by that of a local saint—Hafod Illtyd. In either case this is rare. More poetic and probably more recent in origin, since the building but not the name is indicated on the Ordnance Survey map, is Fox's Bark. Even this continues the older naming tradition, however, for the name roots the farm in its landscape, high on a hill-slope near a tangled wood.

Such names grow out of the land, identifying farms with the hills and valleys, the slopes, pools, woods and marshes of the area. In the process, the occupants of the farms are also identified with place. As the farms change hands, the names live on, absorbing the new owners into the tradition of the place, the tradition of the landscape. In this sense the names are anonymous, effacing the memory of the gener-ations of owners, just as the action of frost, ice, lichen and ivy effaces their sandstone memorials in the graveyards.

By contrast, the modern names in the town represent an attempt to impose personality, to bend the dwellings in a way to the owners' will. The effects are sometimes monstrous and absurd. A nearby house is called Foo Chow, named by retired missionaries who had worked in China. For them the name had some significance, but for aftercomers it is grotesque—'Ugly as a brass-band in India', as Ted Hughes wrote of the introduced rhododendron. Another house was recently named Tuc Tin, one of those puns like Dunroamin and Wit's End which crop up in most lower middle class streets. The house has since changed owners, and the name has been removed. Yet together with the 'rural' names, with their romantic longing for another, impossible way of life, the 'crofts', 'brooks' and woods', and the names of faraway places, Rapallo, Setauket, Cresta, they are the perfect names for our weather-vane culture that spins with every wind.

In William Faulkner's novel *As I Lay Dying*, Anse Bundren, a Mississippi 'red neck' farmer, muses on the nuisance and inconvenience of roads. Men and women, according to Anse, were made 'up-and-down ways' like the trees, because God meant them to stay in one place. If he had intended them to be always on the move, he would have made them 'long ways', like a road or a horse. Consequently, no good can come from a house on a road, for the continual traffic will only make the occupants restless and 'wanting to get up and go somewhere else when He aimed for them to stay put like a tree or a stand of corn'.

Anse is a comic figure. He is a lazy man, and is mulling over a lazy man's excuse for not doing something. Yet beneath the comedy is a serious perception of the way in which settled communities have been breaking up all over the Western world. 'Travel broadens the mind' is a lying proverb, at least as far as much modern travel goes; for the tourist to Europe or America or Africa sees only the surface of things: a week here, a week there, inducing a restless desire and a sense of dissatisfaction, as novelty succeeds novelty. It also goes to producing the confusion of names in the streets of our towns. The list of farm names has a unity derived from a strong community sense of how places ought to be named. The list of house names from the town represents mere confusion which cannot be given any shape or significance, like trying to assemble a jigsaw puzzle when each piece is from a different puzzle.

The list also represents an attempt to assert individuality and a sense of personal freedom, although the result is in fact the opposite. The Australian poet, Les Murray, in a sonnet sequence called *The Boys Who Stole the Funeral*, tells the story of how two boys stole an old man's corpse from the city morgue, and took it back for burial in the remote farming community where he had been raised and where he wished to be buried. The story contrasts city and country values: the changeable, faddish and fashionable, with slow evolution within the continuum of a community and a landscape. One of the boys decides he likes it in the country because it makes him feel free:

> *actually I like it up here   theres space*
> *enough to feel free   I think it takes space*

But that is the modern city way of thinking. '*How can you be free,*' retorts one of the farmers angrily, '*you haven't got a place.*'

Freedom, as the farmer knows, is not the rootless urge to travel, to see more and more, to have no ties; freedom is to have a 'place'—the single word packed tight with implication. For, paradoxically, true freedom is to be rooted, to have associations with a particular farm—or house—which is itself established in a specific landscape. Freedom, together with words like individuality, have shifted in meaning in our society to imply assertion of the naked, petty self. 'Rapallo' was perhaps named by a reader of Ezra Pound or a lover of music, 'Setauket' by an expatriate New Englander, 'Tanglewood' by someone who had enjoyed Hawthorne's *Tanglewood Tales*. In the end it does not matter. The names reach out, jostling one another for attention, by turn trivial or romantic, pompous or absurd. No wonder we float like froth on the surface of a stream. Glaswellt-teg, Pen-y-graig, Werngochlyn; Tanglewood, Setauket, Rapallo.

The Shadow of Aberffraw

What makes a two-hundred page translation of medieval Welsh law, followed by two hundred pages of learned notes, glossary and indices, of interest to us now? This is the second volume in Gwasg Gomer's series The Welsh Classics, and the answer is just that: the *Law* attributed to Hywel Dda is a classic, not just of legal history but of Welsh consciousness, with insight into the past and implications for the future of the nation.[1]

Contrary to what may still be the popular belief, the *Law* as it stands has very little to do with the tenth-century king. A compilation of customary law may well have been made at Hywel Dda's instigation; but law is dynamic, changing in response to society. The earliest surviving manuscripts of Welsh law are from the thirteenth century and consequently reflect, more or less, legal theory then. More or less, because, as Dafydd Jenkins is careful to explain in his excellent introduction, the manuscripts also include some archaic material preserved through the habitual conservatism of the legal mind. Only in this dead law do we get a glimpse of what Hywel's *Law* might have contained. The books as we have them, then, are a hotch-potch of legal material, not the enshrinement of a state system of law. Many of the manuscripts differ in significant ways, and the handy pocket-size of some of them suggests that they were probably reference works carried by justices for consultation during trials.

One thing that must strike the reader unfamiliar with the Middle Ages is how different mentality and modes of perception were then compared to now. Book 1 of the *Law* describes the royal court and the laws appertaining to it. Much of the detail reveals a ritualistic way of life which we have largely lost, and which relates the *Law* to medieval folktale and romance where you find the same delight in description of ceremony and precisely designated forfeits and rights, many of which seem almost surreal from a twentieth-century perspective. There is, for example, the *sarhaed* (compensation) due to the King of Aberffraw (i.e. of Gwynedd) for insult done to him:

> The *sarhaed* of the King of Aberffraw is paid thus: a hundred cows for every cantred he has, with a red-eared bull for every hundred cows,

[1] *The Law of Hywel Dda*, ed. and trans. Dafydd Jenkins (Gwasg Gomer, 1986).

35

and a rod of gold as tall as himself and as thick as his little finger, and a plate of gold as broad as his face and as thick as the nail of a ploughman who has been a ploughman for seven years.

Sarhaed is also due to the queen for such seemingly disproportionate things as snatching something from her hand or striking her. Sudden flare-ups of uncontrollable anger and violence were a common feature of life in the Middle Ages, and are reflected in the literature, from saga to *chanson de geste* and romance. One chronicler reports how a twelfth-century English king kicked his pregnant wife in the stomach in a fit of ungovernable fury, in full view of the court. Under such conditions, elaborate rules of etiquette and laws of compensation may have acted as an important restraint on an aristocracy, especially, whose violent emotions can sometimes seem little short of the psychopathic.

But ritualized behaviour governed the lives of lesser people too. Among the perquisites of the court porter we read in the *Law* that, 'For every load of firewood that comes through the gate he is entitled to a stick which he can draw without holding up the horse, and with his hand on the gate.' While

> From the booty of pigs that comes through the gate he is entitled to a pig which he can lift by its bristles with one hand until its feet are as high as his knee.

Even bearing in mind that pigs in the Middle Ages were considerably smaller than modern breeds, this must have been a feat! Part of the point, of course, is to restrict the porter's natural greed by placing almost impossible limits on the getting of his perks.

Such customary law, however, is not merely a quaint way of doing this. It is based on perception of an order that was believed to underlie even the simplest daily task—an order originating, in part, in a number symbolism which is completely alien to the modern mind. Book 1 of the *Law* ends with a miscellany of triads:

> Three things which it is right for the King not to share with anyone: his treasure, and his hawk, and his thief.
>
> Three things a villein is not entitled to sell without his lord's leave: a destrier [war horse] and honey and pigs.
>
> Three arts a villein's son is not entitled to learn without his lord's leave . . . . clerkship and smithcraft and bardism.

To us, these triads do not represent order but the arbitrary imposition of a pseudo-order on social relations. In the Middle Ages, however, symbolic structures of this kind placed the individual within

36

an important framework of rights and obligations which had ritual significance. Many of the laws begin with the words 'It is right': 'It is right that there be four . . . acres in every toft; four tofts in every shareland; four sharelands in every holding; four holdings in every townland; four townlands in every *maenol*; twelve *maenolydd* and two townlands in every commote.'

At one level this list is merely indicative of the need every society has to structure its affairs, without which there would be no society. But the prefatory 'It is right' indicates a concept of order based on agreed and tried procedures which have a customary and often ancient 'authority' behind them. This is very different from the world we live in where our lives are more and more governed by uncertainty. Major changes can be introduced at the stroke of a minister's pen, so that even when our rights seem clear, we can't be sure that some change in government policy won't alter them radically or even sweep some of them away.

By our standards, medieval society was unjust in many respects, but given its premises, there was a sense in which the individual's rights, according to social status, were clear in law. Peasant unrest in the Middle Ages was often motivated not by an urge toward radical reform, but by a desire to protect customary law—which enshrined their rights—from interference by their feudal overlords.

A fundamental aspect of Anglo-Norman and French society was feudalism, and this clearly influenced Hywel's *Law*. A feudal society operates by a hierarchy of power based on land tenure, with attendant rights and obligations originating in the person of the king. Loyalties are personal—a function partly of a small community. Such an interpersonal structure would be unworkable (at least, so most people assume) in a mass society where the individual's duties and rights are organized in relation to an abstraction, the State. This influences the way law has developed, and our attitudes to it. For in a mass society, justice is administered by an ever-expanding bureaucracy through which punishment of the criminal and compensation (if any) for the victim are enforced in the name of the State. One result of this has been a whittling away of concern for the feelings and what in medieval Welsh law would have been considered the rights of the victim. The State, through its legal officers, fixes the scale of penalties for crimes, from imprisonment to fines, the latter being paid into the coffers of the State, while the victim is usually expected to be satisfied that the criminal has 'paid his debt to Society'.

This would have seemed extraordinary in medieval Wales—for most crimes were, and are, committed not against an abstraction, 'Society', but against an individual. Recognizing this, the law in many early medieval societies, including Wales, based criminal law on a system of compensation payable by the perpetrator of the crime to his victim. He may also pay a fine to the king, for in committing his act he broke the king's peace; but the victim's right to compensation according to social status and the nature of the crime, was a founding principle of law. Thus in Welsh law there are no provisions for gaol sentences, and punishment by execution or exile is limited to certain kinds of killing and theft.

As Dafydd Jenkins points out, the elaborate scale of compensation had the severely practical aim of curtailing blood feuding, by satisfying the honour of the victim, or the victim's kin in the case of a killing. But it also rests on recognition of an important psychological truth: that when a crime has been committed against you, it is not 'Society' but you, the individual, who has been outraged. In a mass society, without extended kinship networks, feuding and vengeance have been largely suppressed. But though we hardly use the word any more, most individuals, nonetheless, have an innate sense of honour, which Julian Pitt-Rivers has defined as

> the value of a person in his own eyes, but also in the eyes of his society. It is his estimation of his own worth, his *claim* to pride, but it is also the acknowledgement of that claim, his excellence recognized by society, his *right* to pride. [2]

It is precisely this 'right to pride' on the part of the victim which contemporary English criminal law largely ignores. The most obvious example, because feminists have made it a cause, is rape. In the Ealing vicarage case, the light sentences given to the rapists, taking remission into account, were widely seen as derisory. For many, the issue centres on the old conservative argument that heavier sentences would act as a deterrent. But this diverts attention from the individual case, where the risible sentences were quite clearly felt by the victim and her relatives to be inappropriate to her—in Welsh legal terms—*sarhaed*, which means both compensation due for injury and the injury itself. In our society the victim of crime is often left feeling helpless and isolated, a passive bystander in a legal process often more concerned

[2] 'Honour and Social Status', in *Honour and Shame*, ed. J. G. Peristiany (Weidenfeld and Nicolson, 1965).

with the welfare of the criminal than the honour of the victim, who is likely to emerge from the court house feeling that her value in her own eyes has not been upheld by society but depreciated.

In Welsh law, rape was treated as a serious crime with heavy penalties in the form of compensation to the victim. This was worked out according to what might seem to us a peculiar legal computation. Nonetheless, it shows insight into the nature and outrage of rape. As Dafydd Jenkins explains:

> The payments to be made by the ravisher are worked out logically. There has been violence: so a *dirwy* [financial penalty] is payable to the King. There has been admitted cohabitation: so the woman's *amobr* [fee due originally on loss of virginity] is payable to her lord. The rape has created a union which is terminated within seven years: so *agwedd* [share of the matrimonial property a woman could claim if her marriage was dissolved before seven years] is payable to the woman; if she was a virgin she has lost her virginity, so that she is entitled to *cowyll* [change of head-dress indicating changed status from virgin to married woman]; and she has been insulted, so that she is entitled to *wynebwerth* [i.e. 'face-value', honour, and compensation for being dishonoured].

A similar scale of compensation exists for other serious crimes, especially robbery, theft and homicide. The *Law* lists 'Nine Abetments of Homicide' which reveal something of the premeditated nature of many killings in the Middle Ages—gang killings and revenge killings—described for example in the Icelandic sagas. Among the abetments are 'pointing out the person who will be killed to him who will kill him, and he is called red-tongued'; 'going to the townland where the person who will be killed is, with him who will kill him'; 'holding the person who will be killed, until he who will kill him comes'; and 'seeing the person killed in his presence, without protecting him'.

If caught and found guilty, the murderer is bound to pay *galanas*, compensation for homicide, in which his immediate kin—father, mother, brothers and sisters—are obliged to contribute at fixed rates. If some of these kin are dead, or if the killer cannot raise his share of the *galanas*, then kinfolk out to the seventh degree can be co-opted into paying a share of the compensation to the victim's kin.

The sense of collective responsibility exemplified here is fundamental to Welsh law. The reason is that honour in early medieval Europe was not individual but collective: if a man dishonoured himself, he dishonoured his family, including his extended family. It is their shame, and it is therefore right that they share in the act of compensation. In law, of course, there is the equally important and related need to involve as many of the kin as possible in order to avoid a blood feud. The injured family have *their* honour to be assuaged, and that is done by payment of an agreed and sufficient *galanas* drawn from the family of the killer—who by sharing in the payment tacitly admit their collective responsibility.

Certain provisions were built into the law of compensation, however, for 'if it happens that the homicide pays his share, there is no right to kill him [i.e. on the part of the victim's kin], even if the kindred do not pay their share'. This recognizes the difficulties the criminal might have in collecting from his relatives; but as for his own share, 'though only one penny be wanting', the compensation is not legally fulfilled and the enemies of the murderer can kill him, without his kin having any claim on the goods they may themselves have paid as their share of the *galanas*, and without any other recourse to law. Despite its legal propriety, this clause sets the scene for a bitter feud, one would have thought.

Concern for the victim is everywhere apparent in the *Law*. Nowhere is its underlying principle more clearly expressed than in the explanation that if a man wounds an animal belonging to another, 'it is proper for the person who wounded it to take the animal to him for medical care until it is healthy, since it is not right for the owner of the animal to labour for the illegality of him who did him wrong'.

This principle was lost sight of, as Dafydd Jenkins points out, by the increasingly centralist legal system of England in the later Middle Ages. It might be argued that growing contemporary interest in 'community service' as a means of restitution for certain kinds of crime is a return to it. But this is still framed by the centralist State's concept of the criminal's 'debt to Society' rather than to the individual he has wronged. Someone whose house has been turned over by a burglar or wrecked by vandals has to pick up the pieces himself. What *sarhaed* is there, or acknowledgement of his 'right to pride' in the criminal's doing community service for someone else in the name of that abstraction 'Society'?

Increasingly there is seen to be a discrepancy between the law and social services' concern with the criminal, and many ordinary people's perception that the rights of the victim are being ignored. Recent public agitation, especially in cases of rape and other crimes of violence against the person, may force changes in the law. It is an irony, as Dafydd Jenkins notes, that certain aspects of Welsh law which were superseded by English law in 1536 may now be introduced as enlightened and innovatory reforms over four hundred years later.

On the lintel of the Central Court in Copenhagen are engraved the words *'Med Lov Skal Man Land Bygge'* (A Nation Must Be Built On Law), *land* here having its root in 'land' but with connotations of 'a people', 'a nation'. It is the opening sentence of King Valdemar's *Jyske Lov* (Juttish Law) of 1241, the first code of law to be written down in Denmark, and contemporary with what Dafydd Jenkins calls the classical period of Welsh law under the great kings of Gwynedd.

Professor Jenkins quotes Goronwy Edwards' observations that two things made Wales a nation in the Middle Ages: the language and the law—the latter being, as Goronwy Edwards put it, 'a potent force, recognized by others as well as by ourselves as marking us off from other people and strengthening our national consciousness'. It is instructive to compare the historical development of Wales and Denmark in this respect. Denmark, a small nation of five millions, has lived up to the vernacular imperative with which *Jyske Lov* begins. Danish is naturally the language of all public transactions and the language of its law. With these keystones, it has maintained itself as a *land*.

The language of the law courts in thirteenth century England was Anglo-Norman, not English, and as Dafydd Jenkins rightly says, 'Since Welsh was the language of the law, the Welsh language had a publicly-expressed dignity which English did not have in England at that period . . .' But the tables have long been turned. Only through the actions of insistent individuals and groups like *Cymdeithas yr Iaith Gymraeg* have the Welsh once more been able to use their language as of right in law courts in their own country—which administer English, not Welsh law.

Those who believe Wales has a future as a *land*, a *cenedl*, even though its life is lived entirely through the medium of English, are unlikely to be swayed by arguments to the contrary. A reading of *The Law of Hywel Dda* more than suggests, however, that if that other keystone of nationhood, the language, *Cymraeg*, dies out, then the experience of being 'Welsh' will be a poor thing compared to that of someone living in the reign of the King of Aberffraw—whether they know it or not.

41

The Anglo-Welsh Tradition

Debate over an Anglo-Welsh poetic tradition has in the past been impeded by the unavailability of the work of poets writing before 1900. Even the sampler published by Raymond Garlick for use at Trinity College, Carmarthen, *Some Early Anglo-Welsh Texts*, contained only nineteen poems and extracts. For this reason, *Anglo-Welsh Poetry 1480-1980*[1] is an important anthology, and is in fact unique in the history of Welsh publishing. As well as a comprehensive survey of twentieth-century Anglo-Welsh poetry, it contains nearly eighty pieces by forty-two poets from earlier centuries, and thus enables the ordinary reader, for the first time, to survey the English-language poetry of Wales.

The editors are naturally eager to justify their belief that the poems illustrate a continuous tradition of Welsh poetry written in English, beginning with a handful of poems from the late Middle Ages and reaching its maturity in the twentieth century. They set out their ideas in a full and interesting introduction, which is itself a contribution to the discussion of Anglo-Welsh poetry. How far they succeed in their argument, however, each reader must judge for him or herself. Reading the poems in the light of their introduction, I eventually found myself dissenting: the poems illustrate an important cultural phenomenon, certainly, but not the one the editors ask us to discern in them.

Raymond Garlick and Roland Mathias define the troublesome term 'Anglo-Welsh' this way: 'The English-medium literature of Wales is conveniently described by the term Anglo-Welsh, the first element of the compound being understood to specify the language and the second the provenance of the writing.' The assumption here and elsewhere is that Welsh poets, through the medium of English, have been able to create a body of verse which expresses *Welshness* to no less a degree than those poets who wrote, and write, in Welsh. Anglo-Welsh verse is therefore part of a national literature as opposed to a provincial one. They support this argument by reference to Anthony Conran's interesting concept of 'seepage' between the two linguistic communities of Wales, which, if I understand the term correctly, implies not a direct, conscious borrowing from one culture by another

[1] Ed. Raymond Garlick and Roland Mathias (Poetry Wales Press, 1984).

but a process of osmosis due to the long and intimate contiguity of the two languages. It seems likely that 'seepage' has taken place from time to time in Wales, but it is extremely difficult to prove, and is unlikely to have occurred on the scale, and with the profound consequences, suggested by the editors. For in their concern to establish the *Welshness* of Anglo-Welsh poetry, they have neglected the first part of the 'Anglo/Welsh' compound. Seepage may indeed have occurred from Welsh to English-language poetry, but Raymond Garlick and Roland Mathias fail to consider the far-reaching, direct and provable influence of English poetry on Anglo-Welsh writers.

They themselves claim that 'wherever, whatever, whoever an Anglo-Welsh writer writes about, what he writes is informed by a Welsh sensibility, by approaches, assumptions, standpoints, perceptions, which differ from those of an American, an Anglo-Irish or an English writer'. Yet in the next sentence they concede that 'in Welsh life in general and in education in particular there is a curious failure to examine the positive and creative rôle, historical and contemporary, of English as a language of Wales. In schools, by and large, it continues to be presented as a language and literature of anywhere else but Wales'. As is tacitly admitted here, English is not just a neutral medium for communication, but a subtle and pervasive carrier of cultural attitudes and values. English words, as inherited by Welsh poets, come steeped in associations with *Englishness*. And here we confront what Australians who face the same problem call the 'cultural cringe'—the innate feeling of inferiority in relation to the English of England and the literary culture which it sustains. For historically the English language has been the prime instrument of Anglicization in Wales, Australia and elsewhere in the old Empire. As the editors themselves seem to admit, the emphasis in schools on the literature and language of *England* has done much to confuse the issue of Welshness for Anglo-Welsh people, and has certainly been concerned in the effacement of the sense of Welsh identity that exists for native speakers of Welsh.

Increasingly, however, Anglo-Welsh writers and intellectuals do not want to acknowledge that the loss of the Welsh language is an irreparable loss to Welshness and Welsh sensibility. As if, after a thoroughgoing conquest, French poets spoke and wrote German, yet claimed that their sensibility as Frenchmen had not been impaired in the process. Yet the inroads of English into Welsh since the sixteenth century, and the increased pressure of an Anglicized education system, have meant that most people's taste in poetry, and their sense of poetic tradition, have been formed on the English model, while the 'cultural cringe' has meant that from the beginning, with one or two exceptions, Welsh poets writing in English have been dominated by what is going on across the border.

This fact is amply illustrated by the anthology, where several of the earlier poems chosen reflect a glad acceptance of the Act of Union and its consequences:

> O Cambria, stretch and strain thy utmost breath,
> To praise and pray for Queen Elizabeth.
>   (Morris Kyffin, *The Blessedness of Brytaine*)

The tendency for English-speaking Welshmen to accommodate eagerly to the needs of their English masters is also expressed nowhere more prophetically than in John Davies of Hereford's *Cambria*, addressed to Henry, Prince of Wales, in 1603:

> We'll root up all our roughs, our heaths, our furze,
> And in their place make grass and cowslips grow:
> We will remove what thy dislike incurs
> And with the mountains fill the vales below . . .

Such commitment to the political ascendancy of England is not surprisingly mirrored in these poets' subservience to the dominant English literary tradition as well. In fact, throughout the anthology with rare exceptions, the touchstone for Anglo-Welsh poetry is English poetry. This becomes clear when, for example, the editors tacitly rewrite literary history to make George Herbert a Welsh poet. Traditionally, Herbert has always been seen as a pillar of seventeenth-century English devotional poetry, and while this may be considered an example of the aggrandizing tendency of a dominant culture to claim as its own what rightly belongs elsewhere, there is nothing in the editors' argument which supports this view. As evidence of seepage from Welsh literary tradition, they adduce Herbert's careful craftsmanship, his delight in intricate verse forms, his use at times of striking compounds ('Christ-side-piercing'), and of *dyfalu* in 'Prayer'. Yet a delight in the craft of verse is equally apparent in Donne, and indeed in Metaphysical and Cavalier poetry generally (compare Herrick, Suckling, Lovelace). And while the image 'Christ-side-piercing' is certainly striking, such compounding is untypical of Herbert's style as a whole, though it is far from uncommon in English Renaissance poetry generally ('tough-thick-rib'd hoopes' [Carew, 'An

Elegie Upon . . . Dr John Donne'], 'steep-down gulphs of liquid fire' [*Othello*], 'sulphurous and thought-executing fires' [*King Lear*]). Likewise, while 'Prayer' is a *tour de force* in its accumulation of similes for prayer, such a device is not limited to the *dyfalu* of Welsh-language poetry, but is part of rhetorical teaching on 'amplification', well-known to European poets since at least the twelfth century through works such as Geoffrey de Vinsauf's *Poetria Nova*. Where there is evidence of *direct* influence from the mainstream of English poetic tradition, it seems unnecessary, at least, to go in search of 'seepage' from a literary culture with which Herbert was clearly unfamiliar.

The editors are right to stress the importance of style here and in their discussion of Anglo-Welsh poetry generally. For where two or more nations share a language, what distinguishes a provincial from a national literature is style rather than themes. Here the parallel between Wales and Australia is more appropriate than the one often made with Ireland and Scotland. The latter have distinctive dialects of English which in the case of Scotland at least has supported a literary tradition descending through Burns to the Scottish Chaucerians of the fifteenth century. Raymond Garlick and Roland Mathias note the existence of an Anglo-Welsh dialect although, as they admit, most Welsh writers—and almost all poets—have drawn, and still draw, on standard English. The parallel with Australia is significant. In both cases, dialect has traditionally been used only for comic purposes, 'serious' writing being undertaken in standard English. This is one function of the cultural cringe which results in a low estimate of one's own working class or colonial dialect, and the urge to write in a mode sanctioned by the 'superior' mother culture. In Australia this has meant until recently a dependence on a prevalent *English* diction and style, often of a slightly outmoded kind—which is a feature of provincial literature.

The same has happened historically in Wales, as the anthology amply demonstrates. So mid-seventeenth-century poet Rowland Watkyns in his poem 'Golden Grove, Carmarthen' writes in a quite specific English tradition of poems in praise of country seats. This has its origin in poems like Ben Johnson's 'To Penshurst', where house and grounds are lauded in a late pastoral mode, combining classical allusion and English topography:

> Though hast thy walks for health, as well as sport;
> Thy mount, to which the dryads do resort,

45

Where Pan and Bacchus their high feasts have made,
Beneath the broad beech and the chestnut shade . . .
                    ('To Penshurst')

Wise Nature here did strive, and witty Art,
To please the curious eye and longing heart.
The neighbouring river Towy doth o'erflow
Like pleasant Nilus the rich meads below.
                    ('Golden Grove, Carmarthen')

Here verse form, diction, imagery, rhetorical commonplaces, and overall tone, are virtually identical. This is not, perhaps, surprising where Watkins is venturing such an essentially English theme; yet even in poems by predominently Welsh-language poets and on Welsh themes, diction, imagery, verse form and the underlying feel for the rhythms of verse are steeped in English literary tradition. So the late-eighteenth-century poet Evan Evans can write in 'The Love of Our Country':

The false historians of a polished age
Show that the Saxon has not lost his rage,
Though tamed by arts his rancour still remains:
Beware of Saxons still, ye Cambrian swains.

The poem contains a patriotic fervour that can be admired by Welshmen now, but stylistically it is utterly derivative from the works of metropolitan English poets like Dr Johnson.

These are not isolated examples. Edward Davies's 'Chepstow: a Poem' is in the tradition of eighteenth-century English rural verse (compare Thomson, Cowper); Evan Lloyd's 'Portrait of a Bishop' is competent satire in the manner of Pope; Iolo Morganwg's 'The Happy Farmer' looks stylistically to the village poems of Goldsmith; Lewis Morris's 'The Fishing Lass of Hakin' is a comic poem in the vein of literary versions of the broadside ballad such as Cowper's 'John Gilpin', and so on.

These poems are all from the early period of Anglo-Welsh verse, and it might be argued that as English became more established in Wales this dependence on English literary tradition gradually died away. In the twentieth century at least, the argument is often made, Anglo-Welsh poetry has emerged as part of a *national* Welsh literature. Yet it may be asked to what extent there is a national identity to express for English-speaking Welsh writers? Unlike Scotland, Wales has never had the usual external signs of nationhood: an ancient seat of government, its own legal and banking systems, etc. Historically the sense of nationhood has been carried by the Welsh language. Take away the language and the cultural tradition it sustains, and what is the difference between the experience of Welsh and Nottinghamshire coal miners, Welsh and Yorkshire hill farmers? Work conditions, social, economic and religious organization are much the same. Only the language pulls Wales in a different direction, and as this declines, increased pressure from English mass culture through radio, TV and the press tend against the existence of a coherent Welsh community and towards a *de facto* acceptance of a provincial, working-class English culture, with a gloss of sentimental 'Welshness'.

This drift towards provincialism is denied by the editors both explicitly in their introduction and implicitly in the rationale behind the anthology. They argue, for example, that Wales's long history provides a depth of association for Welsh men and women, Anglo or otherwise, and that reference to this occurs frequently and naturally in Anglo-Welsh poetry. But how far is this the case, and what assumptions are being made here about cultural continuity? Although it is not overtly stated, Raymond Garlick and Roland Mathias appear to assume a kind of cultural-historical 'seepage' from the past, as well as a more specific poetic seepage from Welsh-language poetry. This is an area of great difficulty. Many allusions to the past in Anglo-Welsh verse appear forced—thrust upon the poem, rather than emerging naturally from the deeper levels where poems are gestated. The editors point out that the outsider will often fail to understand a poem fully 'unless he has done his homework' and read up on Welsh history. The phrase is revealing, for too often one feels that the poets depend on 'homework' themselves. Moreover, until recently, Welsh history has been taught either badly or not taught at all, and the fact is that most English-speaking Welshmen would be as hard put as any 'foreigner' to identify the allusions to Welsh legend, myth and history that crowd some poems. Welsh literary culture has not been successfully transmitted as something alive in the nation's imagination as the Welsh and English languages have exchanged dominance. The history and 'mythology' of English speakers is centred on the mining industry and has its roots in nineteenth-century industrialism and socialism. But this is something south Wales shares with Nottinghamshire, Yorkshire and other regions of England, making it a provincial example of a wider British (i.e. English) social and cultural pattern.

It is not surprising, therefore, that in this century Anglo-Welsh poets are still attracted by English literary models. The editors note, for example, the tendency for some form of nature poetry to predominate in Anglo-Welsh verse, despite the fact that most English-speaking Welshmen live in an industrial environment. They suggest, probably quite rightly, that this reflects the fact that so many mining communities are villages close to unspoilt country. But Raymond Garlick and Roland Mathias go on to make the more dubious proposal that this may also reflect 'the fact that Celtic culture is not an urban one and does not feel the contempt for the countryman reflected in such words as "yokel", "clown", "bumkin", "hick", and their equivalents in other modern European languages'. Firstly the traditional scorn of south Walians for the 'Cardi' shows exactly the kind of contempt the editors say does not exist in Wales. But more importantly, they appear to be intruding again some kind of historical seepage from 'Celtic' culture which, by implication, is a defining feature of modern Anglo-Welsh poetry. Such a tenuous link with the past, surviving social, economic, linguistic and cultural change, seems unprovable. Nor is it necessary, for English poetry since the Romantics has exhibited the same phenomenon: nature poetry co-existing with rapid increase in industrialization. One has only to mention Wordsworth, Clare, Hopkins, Hardy, Edward Thomas, D.H. Lawrence and more recently, Ted Hughes, to realize how significant the tradition is.

Its impact on Anglo-Welsh poetry is clear. In the early decades of this century, poets like Ernest Rhys, W.H. Davies and A.G. Prys-Jones wrote rural verse in the manner of the Georgians. (W.H. Davies is usually classed as a Georgian.) Much of what they wrote is good of its kind, but it is an English kind, as these two examples, which could have come from any of the *Georgian Anthologies*, show:

> He saw far-off the homing crows sail into mottled sky, —
> Saw horse and horseman flag and tire, and trees like men go by.
> (Ernest Rhys, 'The Ballad of the Homing Men')

> Here did his fathers live and pass
>   To slumber after ceaseless toil,
> Sealing beneath the springing grass
>   Their silent epic of the soil.
>   (A. G. Prys-Jones, 'The Ploughman')

Later generations have continued the debt. Alun Lewis's 'All Day it has Rained', for example, assumes a poetic voice with antecedents in the work of Brooke, Blunden and Edward Thomas among others (the latter excluded from the anthology, incidentally, presumably as an English poet):

> All day the rain has glided, wave and mist and dream,
> Drenching the gorse and heather, a gossamer stream
> Too light to stir the acorns that suddenly
> Snatched from their cups by the wild south-westerly
> Pattered against the tent and our upturned dreaming faces.
>
> ('All Day It Has Rained')

Compare this with Edward Thomas:

> It rains, and nothing stirs within the fence
> Anywhere through the orchard's untrodden, dense
> Forest of parsley. The great diamonds
> Of rain on the grassblades there is none to break
> Or the fallen petals further down to shake.
>
> ('It Rains')

Or Wilfred Owen:

> Hour after hour they ponder the warm field—
> And the far valley behind, where the buttercup
> Had blessed with gold their slow boots coming up,
> Where even the little brambles would not yield,
> But clutched and clung to them like sorrowing hands . . .
>
> ('Spring Offensive')

Here is the same quiet, unassuming voice, an English voice, with its restrained diction and rhythm, its attention to natural detail. And it is a voice which lingers in the poems of contemporary Anglo-Welsh writers like Leslie Norris and Gillian Clarke (see Leslie Norris's 'Water' and 'Early Frost' and Gillian Clarke's 'Blaen Cwrt' and 'Ram', for example). In fact a case can be made for the Georgian voice —not merely in its nature poetry—as a major source for what is often considered essentially Anglo-Welsh verse.

There are, of course, other voices in Anglo-Welsh poetry and the editors argue that the first generation of poets to express themselves in English after the spread of secondary education in the 1890s used the language in a way which showed their consciousness of a national difference. As examples they cite Glyn Jones, Dylan Thomas, Vernon

Watkins, Keidrych Rhys and Idris Davies. Here they are on firmer ground, for there is no doubt that these poets did, in varying degrees, use English differently from their contemporaries in England, and that they laid the foundation for what might have become a national Welsh literature in English. Even so, the influence of English tradition on their work should be confronted. Dylan Thomas's style, for example, is often thought, especially by Americans and the English, to be typically Welsh or 'Celtic'. Yet the ebullience of his language, his heavy stress on verbs and nouns accentuated by alliteration and assonance draw on Gerard Manley Hopkins and Shakespeare, and behind them through, perhaps, 'seepage', on the alliterative verse of the English West Midlands of the late Middle Ages. There may also, of course, be indirect influence from Welsh verse via Hopkins, who unlike Dylan Thomas could read, and even wrote, Welsh. But what both poets have done is by-pass the urbane mainstream of English poetry to return to the ground rhythms of Anglo-Saxon speech. Hopkins's 'sprung rhythm', for example, is no more than a re-expression or rediscovery of the rhythmic and alliterative bases of Middle English alliterative verse, and this aspect of his poetry influenced Dylan Thomas profoundly. It is no accident that Thomas's successor in this style is the English poet Ted Hughes.

The last eighty pages of the anthology present the work of poets born in the late 1930s and after. It is here that one must look for those strands which have most recently expressed Anglo-Welshness in poetry, and which may be expected to do so in the immediate future. The selection is wide ranging and includes most poets who began publishing in the 1960s and 1970s. Raymond Garlick and Roland Mathias note that 'there is considerable ground for thinking that younger Anglo-Welsh poets are drawn from a background increasingly separated from an ignorance of the Welsh heritage'—which they associate with the Welsh language. The poems they have selected bear this out. The work of poets in their thirties and forties shows, still, the influence of English rural verse, but it also reveals poets who affect what might be called an 'international' style that is confessional, domestic, sired by late-Romanticism on American poetry of the 1960s, in which the world has shrunk to the autobiographical 'I' and its doings. Such verse is being written in various shadings in the USA, Canada, Australia, New Zealand, England, and is not in any way specific to Wales, except perhaps in that it signals the further dilution of Welsh culture through the English language.

Discussion of a national Welsh poetry in English has often been vitiated by the eagerness to discover a fully-fledged tradition which was there all the time waiting to be recognized. New nations confront the same problem. It is there in accounts of Australian literary history; the desire to have a national literature independent of the dominant mother culture, and the impatience with the long and difficult process of achieving one. There are poets in this anthology who seem to me to express something unequivocally Welsh in an English which no Englishman could have attempted. One is the remarkable Morgan Llwyd from the seventeenth century, a Welsh-language poet who also wrote in English. The other from our century is not Dylan Thomas, but his contemporary R.S. Thomas, who concludes his poem 'Welsh History' this way:

> We were a people, and are so yet.
> When we have finished quarrelling for crumbs
> Under the table, or gnawing the bones
> Of a dead culture, we will arise,
> Armed, but not in the old way.

However, R.S. Thomas identifies the survival of Wales as a nation with the survival of Welsh. Language and culture are not, in the end, separable. It is a position which seems right, though it is one which produces much hostility. This is partly because the notions of English-speakers in Wales about language and culture are filtered through English, which, like any language, is not an impartial medium of communication but a subtle purveyor of assumptions and attitudes. The English are confident that language and culture are separable because, paradoxically, their own are so strongly fused together. The majority of English speakers perceive other cultures only through the medium of English. It is easy then to assume that French 'culture' is somehow separable from the French language. It 'translates'. The degree to which this assumption is prevalent in English-speaking Wales is a measure of how British (i.e. English) we have become. R.S. Thomas's position threatens to tear his own poetry apart; but the opposite looks more and more like a version of H.C. Andersen's story of the king with no clothes.

The Art of Puffing

Kingsley Amis has been back to south Wales—more specifically to Swansea and the Gower—and has not liked what he has seen. With some notes on local colour and *Y Geiriadur Mawr* for the odd Welsh word, he has consequently set about exposing the Wales of the Eighties in his latest novel *The Old Devils*,[1] which was received enthusiastically by the London weeklies and now, with the Booker Prize behind it, is assured of popular success in England. By general consent the satire on Welsh nastiness and pretension is spot-on—what one would expect from the 'old master' as reviewers like to call Amis. There are even Welsh people, Blake Morrison declared in *The Times Literary Supplement*, who will be pleased with it—'For Amis's attack on "false" boyo Welshness keeps alive the notion of a "true" Wales where he [i.e. Amis] might feel properly at home.'

The novel has also been praised for its style: '. . . the verbal texture of *The Old Devils* is richer, more unremitting, than ever before; less, and less prepared, with every clause, to let us slump back into the comfortable old worn *fauteuil* that every novelist hollows out for us sooner or later,' drawled John Bailey in *The London Review of Books* from his own comfortable old worn *fauteuil*. 'Amis's fiction is an acquired taste, the work of a mature artist, weak on plot, all the energy going into style,' claimed an anonymous *Observer* profile. Adding as an after-thought: 'New readers, unfamiliar with his *oeuvre*, may feel puzzled.'

Readers, new or old, who turn from the reviews to *The Old Devils* may well be puzzled—not by anything in Amis's art, but by how such a mediocre novel could be puffed so barefacedly by critics with a reputation.

Its starting point is the return of Alun Weaver to Wales after a career in London as a media personality, second-rate poet and professional Welshman who has lived off, but also in the shadow of, 'Brydan'—a thin disguise for Dylan Thomas. Back home, Alun re-establishes contact with old friends Malcolm, Peter and Charlie, now in their sixties and more or less resigned to a daily round of marital bickering and heavy drinking. The poet's return is not entirely welcome, though, for his friends are equivocal about his success in London, and resent him as a *poseur* and mischief-maker. Their mis-

[1] Hutchinson, 1986.

52

givings are confirmed as, among other things, Alun proceeds to cuckold them one by one—though he draws the line at Muriel, Peter's hard-bitten English wife.

What English reviewers regard as the satire on contemporary Wales, 'that sad Principality' as Anthony Burgess called it in his review of *The Old Devils*, is in fact a pervasive venemous hatred, projected largely through these characters. Muriel, for example, tells a story reported to her by an Englishman who had been laying pipelines 'among the Welsh hill tribes' which illustrates for her what makes 'Johnny Welshman tick'. Her English acquaintance had heard a sermon preached in Welsh in which the minister constantly used what seemed to be the English word 'truth': 'There'd be a flood of bongo-bongo chatter, and then suddenly, truth, and then more monkey language.' When the Englishman asks a native speaker why this was, he is told there is no word for truth in Welsh which has the same force and range of association. 'And if that isn't funny enough for you, he said there is a Welsh word *truth*, same word, spelt the same anyhow, and it means falsehood.'

Muriel is, of course, English and her anecdote might be taken as a reflection of her own chauvinist mentality. But Welsh characters are equally vituperative. When Charlie is spoken to by an American Welshman in Welsh he fails at first to recognize the language, then tries to brush the man aside. 'It had not been fair,' he muses, 'to expect an old soak whose Welsh vocabulary started and stopped with *yr* and *bach* and *myn* to recognize the rubbish when it came at him unheralded in an American accent.' 'Wales is a subject that can't be talked about,' Peter declares. 'Unless you're making a collection of dishonesty and self-deception and sentimental bullshit. That's all you ever hear.'

Put in the mouths of Welsh characters, statements like this deflect attention from the fact of Amis's chauvinism, for anti-Welshness can be presented as a kind of national self-hate, a part of the malaise of being Welsh. But narratorial comment is riddled with hatred of the Welsh in the same way:

> They went outside and stood where a sign used to say Taxi and now said Taxi/Tacsi for the benefit of Welsh people who had never seen the letter X before.
>
> . . . he did a buttering up job on Alun that was a good deal more efficient than might have been expected in a restaurant in a provincial town, even a Welsh one.

> . . . a dark-complexioned man of melancholy, thoughtful appearance . . . a common Welsh type not often noted for either quality.
>
> Glasses were drained, but not always left empty because there seemed to be a feeling that no opened wine should be allowed to remain undrunk, perhaps out of some old Cymric superstition.

And so it goes on. The prepositional phrase 'by here' in Valleys' dialect is referred to as 'a local vulgarism'. When Alun's daughter puts on a fake Welsh accent, it is in a 'quacking local accent' which she does 'efficiently enough though she had never lived in Wales.'

This is not satire but the gibes of a shallow man. In *The Observer* profile mentioned earlier, the author notes that Amis, the rebel of the Fifties, has in more recent years 'hardened into self-caricature as the Great Bullshit Detector' who, like his friend Larkin, rejects with a sneer the Modernist tradition in literature and art and modern jazz—all this coming under the heading 'Bullshit'. 'At the same time,' the profile writer continues, 'he acquired an almost complete set, in mint condition, of saloon bar right-wing prejudices and hallucinations.'

London critics have always been indulgent to the anti-intellectualism and right-wing views of the Movement, partly because they share many of them. If Amis were merely another ultra-conservative member of the Garrick Club, it would hardly matter. But he is also acclaimed by the London literary world as an important English novelist—and no one is going to say otherwise. So the profile writer tries to distinguish between Amis the man and the novelist who 'is too fine an artist to allow [his prejudices] to distort his novels, which are by no means vehicles of self-justification'. For 'Amis stands in the great comic-realist tradition that derives from Fielding—the novel of manners and morals, strong on plot and entertaining dialogue.' (Two paragraphs later, in a passage already quoted, the writer notes that Amis's later fiction is 'weak on plot'.)

None of this will do. Fielding's comedy came from a humane and generous view of human foibles and weakness. Amis, as *The Old Devils* well demonstrates, is rooted in narrow prejudice and intolerance of the kind which thinks shouting 'Fuck off' from a rapidly accelerating taxi unbearably funny (see p. 84). Unlike Fielding, Amis in fact has no moral base for his satire other than his prejudice. *The Old Devils* has been praised for its insight into the decline of Wales as a human, habitable place—'he laments the Europeanisation of Wales', says the author of *The Observer* profile and quotes, for approval, a passage also picked out by Blake Morrison in his review for *The Times Literary Supplement*:

> Where not so long ago it had been hake and chips, bottled cockles, pork pies and pints of Troeth bitter, these days it was cannelloni, paella, stifado, cans of Fosters, bottles of Rioja . . . just like everywhere else.

There is much comment of a similar kind in the novel about bikeys, pub musak, modern youth, the whole food craze, but only at the level of noting their existence and how obnoxious it all is. Amis never gets beyond the surface perceptions of a Colonel Blimp whose annoyance with the present alternates with sentimental reminiscence about the past. Even the praise of a vanished Wales 'of pubs and working villages and Orwellian decency', as Blake Morrison puts it, is sentimental—as Morrison himself recognizes. But it is also a world Amis more than half despises. *Troeth*, in the passage quoted approvingly by Morrison and *The Observer* journalist is dictionary Welsh for 'urine'.

Most surprising of all in the London reviews is the consistent praise of Amis as a stylist—praise which is not merely excessive but demonstrably wrong. Only a friend of the author or someone responding blindly to his reputation, could claim that *The Old Devils* is well written.

In fact, it is badly written, full of careless phrasing, and sylistic ticks like the use of incremental variation to pad out a trivial detail or fact: 'It was likely, it was as good as certain that'; 'As they stood, or with some minor surgery, they were supposed to be, he had striven to make them, his devoutest hope was that they were, the opening section'; 'A train, a particular train, the 15.15 out of Paddington . . .'

When he attempts description, Amis reaches for the nearest set of (preferably double) adjectives: 'Her neat short hair-cut and unadorned black-framed spectacles'; a woman sitting on the floor bends her 'shapely sleek dark head towards the thick shaggy rug'. Or he overloads the sentence with detail which has the evocativeness of a shopping list: 'At her side stood a half-full 40 oz. flask of California Pinot Chardonnay and a brimming blue-glass ashtray with the distinction of having two cigarette-ends burning away in it at the same time.'

In the last example there is an attempt to be witty through the application of ornate language to a trivial fact: 'with the distinction of having two ciragette-ends burning in it'. But this is the manipulation of a stale device such as you would expect from a clever sixth former rather

55

than a 'master of style': 'The coffee and attendant biscuits', 'Having unrestively waited rather longer than strict equity would have entailed', and so on.

There is in fact enough evidence of gratuitously bad writing to suggest that Amis has no interest in style at all:

> . . . what he had said to Sophie just now about her appearance and so on was of course untrue, though it would have been *much untruer*, one had to admit, of most other people he had known that long. [My emphasis.]
>
> What with one thing and another he felt quite pleased with life for the rest of the evening. Pre-eminent among the things there featured prominently and foreseeably the provisional clearance, or seven out of ten, he had awarded the existing portion of *Coming Home*—the sterling anti-trendy title for the complete work he had somehow captured over the last hours.

These are examples of the indirect reporting of characters' thoughts. The solecism in the first and the circumlocution and fuzziness of the second may therefore be defended as a function of characterization. But these traits are endemic to the style of *The Old Devils*, and are also present in narratorial comment and description, as well as in the dialogue which is full of statements like:

> Hey, that's like dead funny isn't it, I never thought of it like that before, but it's like when somebody like a dissident or a minority finds they can't get anywhere through the legal channels so they go round blowing up power stations.

This is admittedly the odious Muriel, but there is little attempt to distinguish the characters through dialogue, and many of their speeches are interchangeable:

> All he's ever said is it's nothing to do with anything and it doesn't mean anything. I'm fed up. He ought to say *something*. I mean about *something*. It gets depressing when a bloke never says anything.

Muriel? No, Sophie. As a result, it is sometimes hard to follow dialogue since one character merges easily into another through the use of the same imprecise, meandering speech patterns.

When Amis does attempt characterization through dialogue it is often perfunctory. Victor, Charlie's homosexual restauranteur brother, goes around like a Kenny Everett character saying 'Horrid little ninny of a wine' and 'the coq au vin is going to be a positive dream'. Attempts to indicate emotion through action are equally unconvincing. Alun, newly arrived in town, bumps unexpectedly into two of his old friends in Victor's restaurant: 'All three men seemed to turn rigid for an instant, then came back to life and motion.' Or again: 'With a small start Rhiannon noticed that the bottle of white wine on the table in front of her was not the same as the one they had started on quite a short time earlier.' This is the symbolic gesture of the comic strip. Even on its own terms, the last example is hardly in character. You do notice when a new bottle of wine is placed on the table before you, and if you come from a hard-drinking literary set as Alun's wife Rhiannon does, you do not give 'a small start' even if you had failed to notice.

But Amis is as little interested in the realization of character as he is in style. Underlying the book is a misanthropic and nihilistic attitude to life which effectively cancels out any curiosity about people, or concern for art. 'Life was first boredom, then more boredom, as long as it was going your way, at least,' muses Charlie who is meant as one of the novel's more sympathetic characters. With its echo of Larkin's 'Nothing, like something, happens anywhere', it illustrates the spiritual bankruptcy that has never been far beneath the surface of the Movement's anti-intellectual stance.

At one point in *The Old Devils* Alun asks Charlie to read the opening pages of a novel he is writing. He does not want him to comment on the style or anything like that, but to act as a 'bullshit detector'. Charlie reads it and against Alun's expectations tells him it is bullshit. It is a pity that Kingsley Amis did not have a friend to do the same for him.

BLUES

Big Road Blues

Coming face to face with a culture you have known only at a distance can be a discouraging experience. Like going back to where you once belonged, the territory is there but the maps you carry are all wrong. Some things are better left to the imagination or memory. The thought occurred to me as we flew in a long arc from Boston via Toronto to Memphis, Tennessee. After twenty years of collecting blues on record and reading all I could on Southern black culture, I was to spend five months in the Mid and Deep South. How well would my imagined world hold up against the real one?

At Nashville we changed planes. It was the beginning of August and I had my first intimation of Southern heat as we filed out of the air-craft. There was a twelve-inch gap between the fusilage and the hydraulic tunnel leading to the airport. Stepping past it, warm air shimmering off the tarmac was like the heat-glare from a furnace, sucking the breath away. But in the air-conditioned transit lounge the intense sunlight and thunderheads punching up into the blue outside seemed unreal, divorced from that second of muggy unbreathable heat.

When we reached Memphis it was sundown and as we set off in an airport minibus, the city cooled like an oven. 'Where to?' asked the driver. I asked for a hotel downtown and he laughed. 'Ain't nothing there.' But he took us all the same to a Ramada Inn and left us with our luggage on the deserted sidewalk. Traffic lights blinked from red to green and back to red again, but at this dead time of the day there was no traffic to control. Downtown seemed to consist of two parallel streets of shops and office buildings that dissolved into slums and vacant lots. From the sealed window of our ninth-storey bedroom I looked down on the street: a few blacks talked quietly in a group, and an elderly drunk stumbled by, whistling a tune whose off-key notes echoed from the empty buildings. The last red sunlight glowed on concrete and brick.

After existing for two weeks in the windowless basement of a dormitory, we found a flat in mid-town, rented furniture from the Acme Furniture Company and began to take bearings. The first thing was to learn to cope with the heat. The Center for Southern Folklore where I worked was thirty minutes' walk from the apartment, yet even in the

61

comparative cool of early morning, my shirt was soaked through with sweat when we arrived. It stuck icily to my skin for hours in the air-conditioned building. At home we discovered that air-conditioning was too expensive and did the best we could with what passed for a draught between the open windows. After a cold shower and a change of clothes it was possible to feel cool for a few minutes, but sweat soon began to ooze from the pores and you were covered again by a thin smear of grease.

The ice-making machine communal to the apartment block became indispensable, disgorging chips of ice into a basin where you could plunge in a jug or bucket. So too did Joe's Liquor Store on the corner, which had a fine display of Bourbon whiskey—two walls lined from floor to ceiling with shelves of half-pints, pints and fifths, a liquid library where I browsed most days, undecided between *Old Crow* ('Generation after generation, men of fame and discriminating taste have enjoyed and preferred this smoothest and mellowest of Bourbons') and *J. W. Dant* ('The unusual and distinctive taste of this unique charcoal perfected whiskey is the result of an old and famous formula, matured and mellowed by natural agents and time in charred barrels'). Or should it be *Rebel Yell* ('Fourteen years before the great victory at Chicamauga, W. L. Weller founded our distillery and produced his first barrel of Bourbon. The whiskey in this bottle is made from the same Southern sour mash recipe that made his Bourbon famous'). And what about Evan Williams, 'Kentucky's first distiller?' How had he found his way to Bardstown, Nelson County, in 1783?

At work I began sifting through hours of reel to reel tape of Delta blues, recorded in the 1960s by one of the Center for Southern Folklore directors, Bill Ferris. The aim was to edit sufficient material for a documentary LP, but the slow process of listening, listening again, and note taking, was not so different from listening to the blues on record at home. What I wanted was to go down into the Delta itself, the triangle of fertile bottomland between the Yazoo and Mississippi Rivers, with Memphis on its base line and Vicksburg at its apex.

Earlier this century the Delta had had one of the highest densities of black settlement in the South and had produced a rich blues style which extends in unbroken tradition from the turn of the century to the present day. I had listened to the Delta blues from the beginning and, in one sense, I knew it better than any other music. 'Yet and still', as they say in the Delta, blues is the music of a people and a culture that is different from my own. Listening to it on record was therefore an act of the imagination in complex ways as I gradually built up a social, historical and human context for a music I could only know as an outsider. To journey into the Delta would be to put my imagined world and all it meant to me to the test.

Highway 61 is a road that features in many blues. It runs from New Orleans through the Delta and Memphis to Chicago and was one of the great routes out of the South for blacks. It was the road we took to the Delta, descending a bluff from the hamlet of Walls into the flattest land I have ever seen. The highway ran for miles with military precision through featureless fields, or rather giant plots of crops, one 'field' ending where another crop began. It was no longer all cotton, for the time had gone when cotton dominated the Delta economy, but there was more of it than I had expected, straggling hip-high bushes with the cotton bolls mostly hidden by leaves. Later in the fall the leaves would be shrivelled to a burnt brown and the bobbed white bolls could be seen for miles like a falling, timeless snow, while on the horizon giant red harvesters moved humped over the fields, sucking out the cotton and shooting it into high-sided wire-mesh trailers.

Sometimes an acrid smell lingered over the cotton where the crop had been sprayed from the air with defoliant. Leaves were a nuisance to the harvesters. Side by side with the cotton were acres of soya beans, the new cash crop of the Delta. Presumably the defoliants drifted onto them as well.

Now and again a hamlet loomed up, perched at a crossroads, its name prefigured for several miles on the communal water tower that hovered on stilts above the countryside. Most were collections of clapboard shacks, some painted white, but others unpainted and weathered to grey. Many were shotgun houses—each room set one behind the other so you could shoot from the front porch through every room to the back, according to the popular derivation of the name. Like most things in Mississippi they had the air of being temporary, with rubbish of all sorts often accumulating in front yards—gutted cars, oil drums, cans, rusting, junked and abandoned. Larger towns like Clarksdale had suburbs with more substantial brick bungalows with neat lawns, where the whites lived. But the outskirts were always the same—one-storey clapboard buildings, many of them short-order cafés, streets cluttered with billboards and poles, criss-crossed with wires. No one was staying, the streets seemed to say, everyone was about to move on . . .

63

I found I liked this. In Europe, several thousand years of history can seem oppressive at times, every inch of the land tied by its names, buildings, ruins, to tradition, everything dragging you back. Temporariness can have its advantages, freeing you into the this-ness of living now. Freeing you, too, in the case of the Delta, into recognition of the transient nature of our lives. In the heat and humidity, under the blinding blue sky, it was easy to believe this flatland would revert to wilderness in a generation, if left to itself. Anything abandoned—an old shack in a sea of cotton—was overwhelmed by creeper choking the chimney stack, by heat and rot buckling the shingles and crumbling the boards.

This somehow went with the undertow of violence. Earlier this century, the Delta had been one of the most violent places on earth. Since the late Sixties, lynchings had come to an end, yet an air of violence remained as if it were implicit, a given condition of the land. ILLEGAL TO SHOOT FROM HIGHWAY said a large sign on Highway 61, but the sign was pitted with shotgun pellets. At Stovall, where Alan Lomax encountered Muddy Waters in 1940 and made the first recordings of him for the Library of Congress, a black man was examining a shotgun outside the isolated post office. The white by his side, eager to make a sale, encouraged him to take aim and fire alongside the open country road. 'Whenever I hear a truck pull up at night, if I don't know the sound of the engine, I reach for my shotgun,' a black told me in Panola County. Shotguns were in evidence sometimes racked across the rear windows of pick-up trucks belonging to whites—good ole boys or red necks, depending on where you stood.

Dead things littered Highway 61, run over and left to rot in the heat. Some were large, deer or dogs with legs stuck stiffly at angles from the bloated belly. Smashed black heaps, a few feathers ruffled by passing traffic, were the remains of black vultures that fed on the roadside carnage. Many were pulped flat on the hard shoulder, run down by someone deliberately going out of his way. With ugly heads, ungainly on the ground, black vultures soared with the grace of eagles high in the Mississippi sky.

All down Highway 61, God and death were companions. 'Jesus Is Lord' said the destination board of a bus outside a brick church in Port Gibson. 'A family that prays together, stays together', advertised a billboard. It was juxtaposed with an advert for life insurance. A few yards down the highway, the red and beige guts of a deer spilled and shone on the tarmac.

64

Back at the Center, I listened through headphones to the voices of older bluesmen as they described a Delta that was the same and savagely different. The region had been cleared of dense primeval forest in the mid-nineteenth century to create one of the richest cotton growing areas of the New South. The labour-intensive crop meant an influx of slaves on a massive scale from the east coast states, and to be 'sold south' to work in the harsher conditions of Mississippi plant-ations was a threat used against recalcitrant slaves in the Old South. Black lives were cheap and remained so well into the present century, finding echoes in the cynical sayings of levee camp bosses recalled by older men: 'If you kill a nigger, I'll hire another one. If you kill a mule, I'll buy another one.' 'Burn out, burn up' (said to men dropping with fatigue from carrying logs all day). 'Fall out, fall dead.'

During Reconstruction, ex-slaves who stayed in the Delta were drawn into a system of debt peonage, 'cropping on shares' as tenants on the old plantations. The system tied black families to the land as surely as slavery, for the tenant farmer was obliged to the landlord for most of his essential supplies, often including mule and plough. These were drawn from the 'commissary' or plantation store, and their cost set against the sale price of the farmer's cotton in the fall. Anything left over was 'profit' for the farmer. In practice, the tenant rarely made a profit and ended the year in debt to the landlord. Even in a good year the landlord who fixed the price of the goods in the commissary, often sold the cotton for the farmer and kept account of mounting commissary debts, could ensure that his tenants came out in debt to him. Poverty, a ruthless police force and a corrupt judiciary made escape difficult in the early years of this century for a black farmer with a large family. The system lingered on well into the Fifties. Older informants on the tapes I listened to had bitter memories of cropping on shares, and the blues I had listened to for years celebrated the struggle of the spirit to survive such conditions.

One late afternoon in September, we drove with friends from Memphis and headed for Tate County just north of the Delta. We were going to the annual barbecue given by Othar Turner on his small farm near Senatobia. The barbecue was a big event in the locality. Several days before, Othar Turner had slaughtered a goat and a pig, and as we entered the yard we were met with the smell of meat being barbecued over hickory charcoal. The yard was beginning to fill up with an assortment of cars and pick-up trucks, as people wandered in from surrounding farms and hamlets. Tate was a 'dry' county, but canned beer and pints of Bourbon whiskey had been ferried across the county line for the occasion, and could be bought at the shack from the older women who had congregated there to chat. In the yard a daughter sold barbecue goat or pigmeat sandwiches, dripping with juices.

As the yard darkened in the evening gloom, someone gave a preliminary roll on a drum and the shrill notes of a cane fife pierced the air over the hubbub of conversation. The party was beginning to take shape. Othar Turner was the leader of one of the last fife and drum bands that were once common in northern Mississippi and parts of western Tennessee. How such bands originated is uncertain, though their roots may lie in early white military bands, whose instruments and rigid march rhythms were wrenched by blacks into their own idiom and for their own purposes. Othar Turner's band consisted of two snare drums and a base drum slung by shoulder straps and played at a slant across one hip. Othar Turner himself played cane fife. The band moved Indian file in a rough circle, the fife reaching out high and clear over the syncopated, polyrhythmic beat of the drums. As the drink passed round, some of the men began to dance, singly, or holding each other by hand or arm in lines of two or three, feet shuffling with and against the beat of the drums, free hands balancing cans of beer or pint bottles of whiskey.

Sometimes the tunes had words, an isolated blues verse sung several times, or a version of 'Sitting on Top of the World', a song recorded by the Mississippi Sheiks, a popular string band in the Twenties; or it might be 'My Babe', a Fifties hit by the Chicago blues harp (i.e. harmonica) player, Little Walter, transfigured, brought back into the fold of an earlier downhome music where the urban 'My Babe' had its roots.

I came back from the shack with a pint of whiskey to be approached by a group of men who wanted to explain that 'Smokey' had meant no insult. Smokey had driven down from Chicago for the barbecue and had suggested to my wife that if she drove back with him to St Louis they could have a good time. Friends and relations had put him right, and now he strolled over and shook hands with a smile. Since many men carried a weapon of some kind, I was glad that my honour had come to no harm.

As we left around midnight, nosing our car onto the dirt road, a sheriff's sedan drew up outside Othar Turner's shack and a white constable stepped out. In a dry county I assumed there was going to be trouble, but he had just stopped by to enjoy himself for a while and to be paid off with a few drinks.

Black music began to take on a new connotation as the months passed. Performances of the kind I had listened to on record were only a part of it. At a party like Othar Turner's, few stood around listening to the music; it was there to be danced to, talked over, while people milled about drinking and laughing, shouting encouragement to the singer. At times someone from the crowd would seize the microphone and sing a stanza or two. The blues was good-time music as well as 'blues', and I came to understand more clearly how it was formed out of the land that stretched flat and vibrant behind juke joint or shack into the dark. *'Tout à fait comme en Afrique,'* remarked a French scholar of Afro-American literature at Othar Turner's band. But it was not just like in Africa.

Yet and still, good-time blues is the lighter side of the Delta's dark coin. 'Do you know what ''on the killin' floor'' means?' asked 'Black Eagle' in the Arkansas flatlands that stretched to the west of the Delta. We nodded. 'Well, I'm on the killin' floor now.' I looked around the sixty-year-old harp player's shack. His wife sat on a lumpy-looking sofa, there was a chest of drawers against one wall, a piece of frayed carpet on the bare boards, a large black-and-white television set where the adverts flickered silently. Skip James had recorded 'Hard Time Killin' Floor Blues' during the Depression in 1931. For Black Eagle, who had played with some of the greatest Delta bluesmen, but had never recorded himself, time had changed little.

In a world of poverty 'Black love is Black wealth,' wrote Nikki Giovanni in a poem that vehemently denies white assumptions that poverty means endless suffering. Her childhood had been a happy one, despite the poverty. At a birthday party for his teenage daughter in his shack near Coldwater, Tate County, farmer and blues singer R. L. Burnside beat out a shattering electrified downhome blues with his band of lead and bass guitars and drums. Apart from the four-foot-high amplifiers, his living room was as bare as Black Eagle's had been. Unlike such a party at home, though, a dozen or more children from toddlers to adolescents milled round the drinking, dancing, laughing adults. When the band took a break, an eight-year-old grabbed his father's guitar, while a younger brother took over the drums. Between them they played a fast blues-boogie with a seriousness and precision that pleased everyone. Later, a little girl squatted and peed on the floor, but nobody seemed to mind. She was lead away by the hand and the mess mopped up.

'Come and see my children,' said a man I'd been drinking with. On a big brass bed in the next room ten or twelve children lay huddled and sprawled asleep. 'This one of ems mine,' he said proudly, picking a child out of the pile like a puppy, 'And this one, and this one.' I admired them, and we went back to the party and the noise and the drink.

Several months in the South, I came to realize, had not so much changed my imagined world as enlarged it. Disembodied voices on a thousand recordings, black-and-white photographs of singers posed or caught in the moment, words on the page, were given depth of colour and movement, were rounded out by sight and sound and the feel of a landscape and community. What I had imagined was real, but lacked that final sense of the contingency of things, the quotidian events that formed a bluesman's life and his songs.

Earlier in the evening we had stopped to eat barbecue at a café and to stock up on whiskey and beer before crossing the county line. Turning off the highway, down narrower and narrower dirt roads, we finally bumped across what seemed to be a field to R. L. Burnside's isolated farm. A large pollen-dust moon had lighted our way, dirt roads glimmering whitely as we passed the humped immobile trunks of trees shrouded in kudzu vines that had strangled and killed them.

Returning to Memphis, the moon had gone down, and we drove along dark roads empty of traffic. On the highway we passed through a hamlet and straight through a crossroads. From nowhere a sheriff's car overtook us and flagged us down. A tall black constable strolled over.

'Is there anything wrong, officer?'

'I didn't see all four wheels stop at the crossroads back yonder.'

'I'm really sorry,' said our white woman driver, 'we didn't notice.'

He leaned one elbow on the car door and peered in.

'Where you folks headed for?'

'Memphis.'

'Memphis, huh.'

He considered giving us a ticket.

'Alright. I guess this time I'll let you slide on by.'

Cover Story

Blues LPs are not usually noted for the quality of their cover design. This is understandable since labels like Matchbox, Roots, Magpie and Agram must run on shoe-string budgets, with little money to spend on artwork. And after all, it is the quality of the music inside the cover that counts in the end. Most labels, under these conditions, fall back on the simple format of a photograph of the singer, where available, set in some abstract design, coloured if you are lucky. If no portrait exists, then a standard alternative is a photograph illustrating some aspect of black life in the South, or Chicago, from the Library of Congress collection. This is the basic formula even of labels like Yazoo that clearly spend much more time and money on cover design.

While lack of funding must be the main reason for poor artwork, another may be the peculiar conditions under which most blues LPs are marketed. The main outlets for the small re-issue labels are specialist mail order firms and a few jazz record shops with a decent blues section. I know of no record *shop* specializing in the blues in Britain.

Under these circumstances, companies do not need to think too much in terms of visual display or packaging in order to attract buyers. The blues record collector will, in general, be familiar with the work of a particular singer or period, and will decide on the strength of that, together with comments in reviews in magazines like *Juke Blues*, whether to send off for a record. I would guess that most collectors buy through mail order firms and never see the cover until after they have bought the record.

This is not a bad thing. In the age of the hard sell, capitalist producers are adept at packaging, tricking out fool's gold to shine like the real thing. Nonetheless, undoing a parcel of four or five LPs on the Earl, Wolf, Roots or Document labels can be a dispiriting experience. The current burgeoning of re-issues from the pre-war period seems to have gone hand in hand with a new austerity in design: a severe black-and-white sleeve dominated by an often blurred photograph, perhaps cocked at an angle, and with liner notes on the back (in the case of Wolf and Matchbox) reversed out in white on black. The impression is funereal and at odds with the music.

As I have suggested, this is less true of specialist labels in the States such as Mamlish and Yazoo, but with more money to spend there is still surprisingly little attempt to relate cover design to the expression of the music. Portrait photographs or paintings from photographs dominate, as on Yazoo's double albums of Blind Lemon Jefferson and Blind Blake, where the centrepiece of each cover is a painting based on the more than well known Paramount publicity photographs from the 1920s.

Exceptional are some of the covers commissioned by Yazoo from R. Crumb, the Sixties' 'alternative society' cult cartoonist. His caricature style works well on the hokum LPs *Please Warm My Weiner* (L-1043) and *Can't Get Enough of That Stuff* (L-1051) where the gross, over-blown 'big fat mamas' with short skirts and bulging bosoms, leered at (on *Please Warm My Weiner*) by two lascivious thick-lipped street singers, parallels pretty well the endless nudging sexual innuendo of the hokum boom of the late Twenties. But R. Crumb's style is limited, and on the Memphis Jug Band double album (L-1067) he falls back on a 'portrait-painting' of the band for the front cover, and a series of not particularly amusing caricature vignettes for the back, illustrating individual songs—'Gator Wobble', 'Cave Man Blues' etc.

For all of these reasons, I doubt whether most record collectors give more than a casual glance at the sleeve when they take a record from the shelf. But one exception for me has been the cover artwork of Nick Caruso on the double albums issued by Chess in their Blues Masters series. These, too, depend on the portrait of the singer but, almost in every case, Nick Caruso wrenches the well-known faces out of context, into a dramatic fantasy world which may seem at odds with the known lives of Chicago blues singers in the Fifties and Sixties. For this reason, however, the covers force you to stop and look more closely and to think about the relation of the image to the music. In fact, Nick Caruso's designs are an interpretation of the music, providing visual symbols for the music's inner energies and compulsions.

The Howlin' Wolf album (6641 538), for instance, shows the Wolf stepping into the cockpit of a World War II fighter, dressed in pilot's flying gear of the period and with an acoustic guitar slung like a gun across his back. His face is lit by a bright light from inside the cramped cockpit. Right hand on the windscreen, he reaches back and towards you, stretching out his left hand as if to give you a lift up into his world. Goggles raised on his forehead, he has a broad grin.

The plane's nose is steeply banked up towards centre-left of the picture, into a flaming dawn. A wolf, in silhouette, howls, head back, at bottom left. Turn the album over, and a dawn-pink light in the lower right of the picture fades off into pale sky-blue. A fighter loops and drifts away from us. The sky is filled with song titles, as if made out of vapour trails.

On his album (2ACMB-203), Muddy Waters is shown in formal morning dress. Across his breast is a pink sash with two stars or crosses like ambassadorial awards from foreign powers. But he sits on an old tree stump by the side of a country road, top hat and kid gloves in his left hand, while with his right he thumbs a lift. On the ground, between his legs, there is a guitar case covered in travel stickers— London, Paris, Germany. The road is not an important road; it is going nowhere in particular. It is autumn; leaves on the trees are bright yellow and red; a few lie scattered at his feet; tarmac is crumbling at the edge of the road.

On the reverse side, a billboard announces the titles of the songs on the album; but there is no traffic, and no one to read them. On the front cover, Muddy Waters looks directly at you as he hitches a ride. But his look is equivocal; you can't decide if he is smiling or not.

The Little Walter album (2ACMB-202) is even more surreal. Little Walter is dressed in natty evening wear—cream-coloured jacket, brown bow tie, brown cummerbund and trousers. He has a large pink flower in his buttonhole and a pink handkerchief in his breast-pocket. Little Walter is standing at an elegant, polished bar, right elbow on the bar, left hand firmly placed on the top of an expensive, ornate bar stool. In his right hand he holds a harp (i.e. harmonica), and two more are scattered on the bar by the side of an empty cocktail glass.

But the right-hand side of the bar merges with a sand dune, and Little Walter is standing with it, on a tropical desert island. Driftwood and a rock lean against the near end of the bar; another bar stool is half buried in drifting sand. The singer, set further back in the picture than Howlin' Wolf or Muddy Waters, is trying to look casual, one leg elegantly crossed over the other; but the shoulders are slightly raised and hunched, as if tensed, and the face looks grim and straight at you.

The back cover shows foreshore sand, stones, a dead starfish, and an empty whiskey bottle, cork at its side. The bottle contained a message on a much-folded scrap of paper, which has been read and thrown down in front of the bottle. The message is the titles of the songs on the album.

To take one last example. J. B. Lenoir (2ACMB-208) is presented bathing in a natural pool in a glade. Water cascades over a rock, splashing his chest. Harps, a guitar, clothes, are scattered around. He looks up at you with a bright, challenging grin. He is having fun and dares you to stop him. At bottom right, the face of a beautiful woman is seen underwater. It is not clear whether she is looking up at you, about to surface, or whether she is drifting, dead.

The back cover centres on a close-up of a forked tree trunk. On each fork is carved a heart, with the titles of the album's songs inside the hearts. A hat and coat have been thrown over a notice board which partially reads 'Viola[tors] will [be] Prosec[uted]'.

Divorced from his *milieu* in the post-war ghettos, each figure is presented in a world which externalizes what the artist has perceived as the inner truth of the singer and his songs. The covers are emblematic: Howlin' Wolf the fighter ace, the confident loner, who flies solo, not in squadrons; and yet he is with you, reaches out to pull you on board. Introducing one of his songs recorded in a club, Howlin' Wolf says: 'Thank you very much. You are my people; you made me; and I'm gon' howl for you.' Then the band starts into the song to enthusiastic calls from the audience. Nick Caruso's cover painting enacts in fantasy that myth of the lone wolf, the tail-dragger, who is at the same time the hero—the ace fighter/singer—of his people.

A similar self-assertiveness and confidence is there in the artwork on the J. B. Lenoir cover. Ignoring property rights (of whites), bathing where he likes, an emblem is created for the aggressive songs of the Fifties like 'Don't Touch My Head' and 'Eisenhower Blues'; while the submissive, perhaps drowned, woman in the pool symbolizes the sexual confidence and bragging of blues like 'Man Watch Your Woman' and 'Mama Talk to Your Daughter'.

But the obverse of this was still the poverty and uncertainty of ghetto life which touched all these singers and which also recurs again and again in the songs. In Nick Caruso's cover for the Muddy Waters album, the singer may be an 'ambassador' for the blues, touring the capitals of Europe and 'decorated' for his services to the blues; yet compared to the Rolling Stones and other white rock groups who made vast fortunes, but who could scarcely have existed without Muddy Waters and his *confrères*, he is still an obscurity—the great ambassador who has to hitch a ride, whose greatest songs are advertised on billboards down empty country roads.

With Little Walter dead at thirty-eight after a hard-drinking, violent life, the clash of images on the cover becomes more extreme again. On harp, Little Walter is the great stylist of the late Forties and Fifties. This is made emblematic in the stylish clothes, the expensive bar. But at the same time he is marooned, all washed up. His songs and his extraordinary harp solos are messages in a bottle that are found and thrown away. The tensed shoulders, the narrowed eyes with their deep, hard look are those of a man who knows he is for it; that there is no way out.

I assume that the main audience for these Chess double albums has, from the beginning, been white. What Nick Caruso does with the covers for the white listener, is to make him take stock of his own relationship to the music which was not sung for him, by musicians who were at once grand—ambassadors, fighter aces; and who at the same time often had their backs to the wall—owners of nothing, hitch-hikers, swimmers in other men's pools, marooned. The covers are a reminder and a warning that no matter how much you might enjoy the music, it comes from a world that can never entirely be yours.

Afro-American Music in Britain

Afro-American music has had such a thoroughgoing influence on European popular music since the First World War that it is no longer easy to feel surprise at the phenomenon. Yet it *is* surprising that a musical tradition so different from anything in Europe should have been so influential. This influence has been particularly strong in Britain where first jazz, then blues instigated what amounts to a revolution in musical sensibility, to a far greater extent, I believe, than on the Continent. The reasons for this are complex, though an important one is clearly language: the fact that the USA and Britain share a common language despite cultural and dialectal differences. This alone makes the blues which, unlike jazz, is heavily dependent on the word, more accessible to an English listener than to one from France or Germany. Yet in itself it is not an adequate explanation of why Afro-American music made such easy inroads into culture here. To discover this, one has to look to the social and cultural changes which occurred during the industrial revolution of the nineteenth century.

Most significant is the rapid change from a rural to an urban environment which accompanied industrialization and which effectively destroyed English folk culture in all but the remotest parts by about 1914. For a culture with its roots in a rural community rarely survives transplanting to an urban, industrial one for long.

As early as 1800, William Wordsworth had observed the effect of the destruction of a rural folk culture on the deracinated urban proletariat. In the Preface to *Lyrical Ballads* he wrote that

> a multitude of causes unknown to former times are now acting with a combined force to blunt the discriminating powers of the mind, and unfitting it for all voluntary exertion to reduce it to a state of almost savage torpor. The most effective of these causes are the great national events which are daily taking place, and the increasing accumulation of men in cities, where the uniformity of their occupations produces a craving for extraordinary incidents which the rapid communication of intelligence hourly gratifies. [1]

Wordsworth goes on to castigate the 'degrading thirst after outrageous stimulation' which he saw in the cities, a thirst which in

---

[1] Preface to *Lyrical Ballads*, ed. H. Littledale (Oxford University Press, 1911, repr. 1931).

74

our own century has reached a proportion beyond his worst fears. In such a context folk music cannot flourish. Like other folk traditions it is open to change, and can absorb influences, but only gradually. Rapid change, of the kind we live with today, destroys the continuum of beliefs, customs, habits between the generations upon which a tradition depends.

In nineteenth century England, the folk culture was replaced as Wordsworth perceived by a meretricious popular culture the basis of which was change, the urge toward the new and the fashionable. Song writing became as a result more and more the province of 'professionals', who churned out lyrics for the music hall and in the form of broadside ballads. Songs were being written *for* the people rather than emanating from among them: a distinction which is fundamental to the difference between a popular and a folk tradition. In the process, popular lyrics became more and more remote from people's lives, creating an unreal world of shallow comedy or sentimentality. Sentimentality especially substitutes the idea of an emotion for the experience, and when it becomes pervasive, as it has done in the popular music of the nineteenth and twentieth centuries, it creates a shadow world of debased romanticism at odds with the lives people lead. This is different from a folk tradition where a song, though it may be modified by formal convention, or heightened by imaginative licence, almost always has its roots in the experience of the community. In traditional culture sentimentality, of the kind endemic in the popular music of the industrial nations, has little place. Instead of creating an unreal and unrealizable world, it celebrates life as it is and provides an imaginatively fulfilling experience for singer and audience alike. Life and art are not set at odds but are synthesized in poetry.

The lyrics of pop music on the other hand rarely achieve the status of poetry. A poem in high art or in folk tradition is the product of someone's dedication to art. In folk tradition, especially, it is the product of both personal and communal energies, for the imagery of a poem or song will, as often as not, have been honed over several generations to a perfect, functional expression of a feeling or experience common to the singer and his community. A singer may add to the store of traditional images, but it will be in full knowledge of the tradition—something patiently learned over many years. [2] Such a folk poetry changes,

[2] The classic accounts of this process are by Milman Parry, *The Making of Homeric Verse*, ed. Adam Parry (Oxford University Press, 1971) and Albert B. Lord, *The Singer of Tales* (Harvard University Press, 1960).

but the change is slow, and what is old may be as valued as much as what is new. Pop music does not and cannot operate like this, for it depends on the new. Last year's Top Ten has lost its lustre and is discarded. Language is consequently not so important and is downgraded, since the rapidity which with songs come and go means that *cliché* is gladly substituted for poetic image, its function being nominal.

Such music does not stimulate the listener's feelings and imagination but rather deadens them, depending on the constant illusion of the new in order to maintain interest. This is why jazz in the 1920s and 1930s was such a revelation in Britain for successive generations of youngsters. It provided a release into a new understanding of rhythm, new possibilities of self expression, though this was strictly musical since jazz lyrics are often as banal as those of pop music, representing at best an attenuated blues tradition. The most thoroughgoing musical revolution in Britain was in the 1960s and 1970s and had its roots in blues rather than jazz. For despite the 'traditional' jazz boom of the post-war years under the influence of revivalist musicians like Bunk Johnson, George Lewis and their British imitators, jazz remained by and large a cult following—no matter how large that following may have been at times. 'Trad' jazz was not absorbed into the mainstream of popular music, its purveyors attempting as far as they could to imitate closely what they understood to be the original. Those like Humphrey Lyttleton who evolved beyond traditional jazz quickly lost in popularity. The various developments in modern jazz remained in Britain a minority pursuit, as jazz itself became more of a concert art, technically too complex for more than a few to be able to play.

Afro-American folk music, however, is different in that its basic harmonic progressions are simple and the instruments associated with it—guitar, harmonica—cheap or, like the piano, comparatively available. As a music, it provided an opportunity for direct participation on a scale beyond the scope of jazz. The first signs of this were inconspicuous: *ad hoc* groups formed from the personnel of trad jazz bands, playing ballads and blues in intermissions or to provide variety during a concert. A few of these 'skiffle' groups were recorded and band leaders like Ken Colyer and Chris Barber found sales competing with their straight jazz performances, causing Chris Barber's banjoist Lonnie Donegan to launch out on his own career as leader of the most successful skiffle group of the period.

The line-up of such groups was similar to that of black string bands of the 1920s, such as Gus Cannon's Jug Stompers and the Memphis Jug Band, though neither the audience for skiffle, nor many of its performers, would have been aware of this at the time. Acoustic guitar, banjo, washboard and tub or double bass provided simple accompaniment to ballads such as 'John Henry', 'Frankie and Johnny', 'The Grey Goose' and other more blues-based songs. Like the jug bands, the repertoire was eclectic and included songs from white tradition as well.

This music, on the surface so alien to the world of young, white, urban Europeans, provided nonetheless an important form of self-expression. Among jazz and skiffle enthusiasts of the 1950s, 'improvisation' was a cult word. It was believed to be the touchstone for the spirit of Afro-American music and as such the key to a spontaneous art denied by Western musical tradition. Knowing little of the tradition of black American music, but knowing they could express a part of themselves through its rhythm and song in a way denied them by the mainstream of their own culture, homemade skiffle bands burgeoned by the thousand. And the fact that they *were* homemade, even to instruments like the washboard and tub bass, is important. Ever since Modernist interest in African art in the 1910s, African and Afro-American cultures have provided successive generations with a criterion for a return to the direct expression of emotion. In terms of popular culture this culminated in the beat/rock music of the 1960s which, unlike the more 'songster'-based skiffle of the previous decade, looked directly to the urban blues of Chicago, Detroit and Oakland— to singers like Muddy Waters, Howlin' Wolf, John Lee Hooker and Elmore James. Rock music, like its blues roots, was more aggressive, more openly in revolt against the values of society; something which expressed itself in the band line-up—the exchange of electric for acoustic guitar, of heavy off-beat drumming for the washboard. It is there too in the often aggressive nature of the lyrics, in the strutting sexuality of Howlin' Wolf's performance of 'Little Red Rooster', for example, which was successfully recorded by the Rolling Stones.

The blues had such influence partly at least because of the 1960s Welfare State generation's need for a music which, unlike Tin Pan Alley, expressed real experience. It reflects the need of the young to suffer, if only vicariously through the songs and experiences of others—experiences of a kind an affluent society attempts to dispel or at least suppress. Hence, too, the urge to explore sexual prowess, not sentimentalism, which was all the music of a mass culture had to offer.

Not surprisingly, perhaps, as a result, there is a lack of conviction about rock versions of the blues. The Rolling Stones' recording of 'Little Red Rooster', for example, shows a consistent diminution in power compared to the version recorded by Howlin' Wolf.[3] Mick Jagger's singing is competent and pleasant, but it is 'about' the red rooster despite the first person presentation in the song ('I am the little red rooster . . .'). It comes over as something learnt, a performance. In Howlin' Wolf's recording for Chess in 1961, the rooster's strutting sexual prowess is *enacted* as we listen. The difference is cultural: in blues tradition the rooster is a symbol of male sexuality and boastfulness. Wolf's audience would have been familiar with this, just as most of them would have been familiar at first hand, as Howlin' Wolf was himself, with the farmyard bird and its ways. For working-class teenagers from London, however, the rooster is remote—something capable of conceptualization but not experienced.

This alone, however, does not account for the thinness of Mick Jagger's performance. There is the difference in style which is fundamental. Mick Jagger keeps close to the basic melody and beat, and because of this his recording is rhythmically rather predictable. Howlin' Wolf's voice—apart from its sheer bite and force, its rich gravelly texture which was cultivated by Mississippi Delta singers—has a different, more incisive sense of timing. The voice moves in and out of the melodic line, with and against the insistent beat of the band. There is the same difference of approach in the work of the lead guitarists. Both use open tuning, and a slide on the treble strings, to achieve a repetitive whine which underpins the sexually suggestive mood of the song, but the Rolling Stones' guitarist is not satisfied with a simple statement, he becomes over-elaborate, cannot resist the urge to embellish, and is in danger of a kind of self-parody as a result. He, like the singer, is standing outside the music, performing something learnt, not enacting something out of his own experience and that of his audience. The result is a dilution of the original for consumption by a white adolescent audience.

There is irony, of course, in the fact that few who responded with enthusiasm to the Rolling Stones' recording would have been aware of its blues roots, or would have appreciated Howlin' Wolf's version if they heard it. Despite the immense debt of rock music to the blues, only a minority has felt impelled to go behind the white imitation to its

[3] These recordings are readily available on, e.g., *Howlin' Wolf*, (Chess Blues Masters 6641 538) and The Rolling Stones, *Get Stoned*, (Arcade Records ADE P32).

source. This is because although rock music changed British popular music in radical ways in the 1960s and 1970s, it was still part of the musical culture of mass urban society. It is one of the peculiarities of pop music in this century that it has consistently fed on folk music in its restless search for new musical crazes. Blues, gospel, zydeco, reggae and country music have all been drawn into its vortex, to be used, manipulated and abandoned. In part this shows awareness of people's unsatisfied need for the genuine, their urge toward the direct expression of emotion. But a folk tradition does not flourish in new soil, and the packaged version that reaches the mass market and which seems to hold out the real, actually only offers shadows.

Even the genuine music is manipulated to the same end. In Britain, probably the most well-known blues singer is Robert Johnson, not because his recordings are great performances and historically significant—which they are—but because Columbia has until recently promoted them in two albums which have been given nationwide advertisement and distribution. Almost anyone interested in rock music will possess one or both of these albums, while, for example, the Library of Congress field recordings from the same period (the late 1930s) have been issued by small specialist companies and are known to only a handful of collectors. Many of the performances on these albums are as fine as anything by Robert Johnson, but his commercial recordings conform more closely to the tailored expectations of young whites, a tailoring created and nurtured by the large mass market record companies.

Yet the specialist companies exist, catering for a minority interest in the blues which is insignificant in terms of the mass market, though noteworthy as an example of what happens when the stable patterns of a culture break down. Desire to escape from the 'savage torpor' which a mass society induces has led many to create a kind of personal culture out of the resources available to them, and for some this has meant commitment to Afro-American musical tradition. This involves an act of imagination, since the music comes from a very different *milieu* to their own. It is also a situation cross-cut with ironies. The white European may see the blues, rightly, as the direct expression of emotion by a coherent community, but it is one he could never belong to for a complex of cultural and historical reasons. Moreover, since that coherence was circumscribed by racism in the historical South, its positive qualities may seem less than attractive to a contemporary black. The final irony is that vicarious experience of black music by

79

the European white isolates him still further from his own culture, since few among his acquaintances are likely to share his commitment. Afro-American music thus opens a door for the white European, but it is one that he can never pass through to say that he belongs.

Shot the Innocent Man

In 1929 a man called Charley Lawson shot his wife and five children in North Carolina, then turned the gun on himself. It happened near the family home of two brothers, Bill and Earl Bollick, who played guitar and mandolin and sang country music together as The Blue Sky Boys. Bill and Earl made a song up about the killings, 'The Lawson Family Tragedy', which they recorded many years later in the 1970s.

In the South there was nothing unusual in this. Both white and black musicians made up songs as a matter of course about events in their communities—often disastrous ones like the Mississippi flood of 1927, or drought, the ruin of cotton crops by the boll weevil, a train wreck, or children burned in a school-house fire. Sometimes, too, they sang about the intrusion of terrible murder, like that of the Lawsons, into their small rural communities.

The Blue Sky Boys' song is a ballad which, in a traditional way, mixes known facts about the killings with the singers' imaginative reconstruction of them. The murders had taken place on Christmas Eve, and this is the first fact mentioned. To the community it was a mystery: 'no one knew what caused him/To take his family's life'. The singers repeat what is known or surmised: 'They say he killed his wife at first'—but then, in ballad style, feel free to invent the imagined pleas of the children:

> Oh daddy dear don't kill us here,
> For we're not prepared to die.

The words are traditional and appear in several ballads but they express an important concept for a Southern Baptist community—the awfulness of sudden death, that leaves you unprepared to face God.

The song then switches to the killer, with understanding of the mind that could snap and carry out such acts. He was a 'raging man', he 'could not be stopped', even by the cries of his children, so

> He kept on firing fatal shots
> Until he killed them all.

Now the song reverts to direct speech; imagines the last words of the father as the rage subsides and he faces what he has done:

'Shot the Innocent Man' is the title of a murder ballad by Cliff Carlisle.

81

And now adieu kind friends and all
You'll see me again no more;
One fatal shot into my breast
And my troubles will be o'er.

The next stanza changes mood again, with a wry comment that at least Charley Lawson has saved everyone the trouble of taking him to gaol and himself the expense of legal fees ('No lawyer will he pay'), together with a reminder that, for this fundamentalist community, moral responsibility can't be evaded by suicide:

He'll have his trial in another world
On the final Judgement Day.

The ballad ends with the shock to the community, its sense of help-lessness, and with the burial of the entire family 'in a crowded grave' —while in the tradition of country music sentimentality, angels look down, urging

Come home, come home, my darling one
To the land of peace and love.

Mass killings are not, of course, as rare as might be supposed, though in Britain people have tended to associate them with the United States rather than our own more 'peaceable' society. The Hungerford massacre and recent multiple family murders have changed that perception of ourselves, however.

Yet reading reports of these events in the press brought 'The Lawson Family Tragedy' and other Southern ballads to mind, for while mass killings are given wide coverage by the media, there is a superficiality about the reporting which is disturbing.

Four recent examples illustrate this. The most sensational was the shooting of 16 people in Arkansas, 14 of whom were members of the killer's family. The timing of the killings—Christmas—and the bloody scene discovered by the police at the home, are strongly remin-iscent of the Lawson murders. According to *The Guardian*, 'Unopened presents were scattered across a blood-stained carpet; one body was found under the Christmas tree and another close to a Nativity scene.' Two years earlier, a young woman (also killed) had accused the killer of 'sexual advances', and that was enough for *The Daily Mail*: 'Reject-ed lover's rampage kills 16' was its headline—though *The Guardian* reported more cautiously that 'Apart from this there was no indication of motive in the killings.'

82

In reports of this kind, it is obligatory to ask neighbours what sort of man the killer was. 'Neighbours described Simmons as a rather strange character who was not well known to them.'

A few days later a man killed 7 members of his family in Iowa, then shot himself. Police theorized that it might be a 'copycat' killing but admitted that 'We have no motive—no vague indications.' Neighbours were more forthcoming than in Arkansas and hinted at a background of mental illness, and of the killer's penchant for firearms.

In Ulster recently, a man shot dead his wife and two children, then, again, turned the gun on himself. A police spokesman said: 'There is no indication of any trouble in the family and we have no idea how this happened.' Neighbours could only say that the murderer was 'quiet'.

In Wales a man battered his wife and daughter to death, then drowned himself. Police 'had no idea of the motive for the killings'. A former employer said the killer had been depressed, but added: 'He did not seem that sort of chap.' Neighbours described him as 'very quiet'.

In each instance there is the evidence of the blood-spattered corpses, but there is also a deep sense of mystery, as if we stare into brilliant light and see nothing; for three of the murderers killed themselves without leaving a hint of their motive, while the fourth, in Arkansas, sat in gaol and refused to speak.

No doubt criminologists and psychiatrists have amassed large amounts of data and theorized extensively about such events, but once the journalists have drifted away, most of us hear no more about them —they have ceased to be 'news'; and we are left with ill-defined feelings of bafflement and defeat.

This must be true especially for the community where the violence occurs, where a network of day-to-day relationships and apparent certainties is torn apart. At such times, the failure of popular culture to concern itself with life rather than yearning and make-believe, becomes clear. For though it existed once, we no longer have a song tradition within communities which can deal with such experiences. We have simulacra of violent events on television and video, but these are generalized, the characters mere vehicles for the violence that unspools before the passive eye and which is the real justification for the film.

The ballads of Southern tradition are different. Not mass-produced for a mass audience, they were composed within the hamlets and townships by singers who often knew the protagonists and who sang about them partly because, as Robert Lowell wrote in the 'Epilogue' to *Day by Day*:

We are poor passing facts,
warned by that to give
each figure in the photograph
his living name.

The adjectival emphasis on '*living* name' is important. For the ballad-maker is not concerned with 'naming' in the sense of the archivist or historian. His job is to come at the *subjective* truth of a named individual at a moment of catastrophe—that person's inner experience which usually cannot be known in a factual way; something which explains the thinness of so much 'news'.

To do this, the ballad-maker as poet, takes liberties, draws on tradition, invents; and the subjective truth he arrives at will be important for his audience, not only because it memorializes the protagonists but because his song enables the community to come at an imaginative understanding of violence and its intrusion into their lives.

Moreover, because the ballad uses discontinuous narrative, the ballad-maker often achieves a striking compression, a Cubist-like, multi-planed view of a killing—introducing the killer's point of view, as well as that of his victims and the community.

This too has a social function which is rarely fulfilled by the media, where a murder is either reported as 'objectively' as possible or presented as a sensational polarization of savage killer and innocent victim. The former has an abstractness which leaves the reader indifferent—it is yet another news item; while the latter appeals without shame to our basest instincts.

The ballad-makers never forget the ethics of killing, but their attitude to those involved is more nuanced.

In 1931, a black singer, Kid Coley, recorded 'Claire and Pearley Blues'. It is unusual, as blues-researcher Paul Oliver has pointed out, in that it is a blues in form but a ballad in content. It is about the murder of Claire and Pearley who were friends or good acquaintances of Kid Coley. His song is ''Bout two girls I really knows well'; and their deaths obviously moved him, because he goes to some lengths to impress on his audience that what he is singing is the *truth*: 'I haven't composed it wrong', he says in the first verse, and he repeats this at the end, in a traditional signature-verse: 'Now if anybody should ask you who in the world wrote such a song, so lonesome and so blue . . ./Tell them that it was Kid Coley and he never composed it wrong'—adding as a coda, 'And it was no lie'.

What Kid Coley narrates is the story of a brutal murder. One Friday night, Claire and Pearley go to bed as usual, not knowing that in the small hours Matthew Kelly will force an entry through their back door and kill them. Matthew Kelly carries a butcher's knife 'some dirty work to do', and as he makes his way through the house, he sees a hatchet which he takes up, saying: 'I swear I'm gonna fix both of you two.' When he comes to the bedroom, he buries the hatchet in Claire's head and presumably (though it's not stated) kills Pearley with the knife.

The song moves stanza by stanza from the sleeping girls to the killer on the prowl and to their final confrontation in the bedroom. Our response has been carefully controlled to ensure that we sympathize with the girls. They are referred to only by their first names, while the murderer is distanced by the use of his full name; and while Claire and Pearley lie innocently asleep, the killer is alert, involved in a *planned* crime ('dirty work to do') in which he takes a vengeful pleasure ('I swear I'm gonna fix both of you two').

Once the murders have been committed, however, there is a sudden shift. Matthew Kelly's arrest, trial and sentencing are passed over, and the song juxtaposes the brutal axing of Claire with her killer's last moments:

> Matthew Kelly walked to the electric chair with his hair combed
>   out in a curl so lonesome and so blue,
> Matthew walked to the electric chair with his hair combed out
>   in a curl,
> Try on a brand new suit of clothes Matthew said: 'It'll be
>   the last I try on in this world.'

Up to this point, the story has been a simple one, but while we are never allowed to forget the horrific nature of the crime, we are now confronted with something close to admiration for Matthew Kelly as he prepares to die. The phrase 'so lonesome and so blue', in line one, occurs in previous stanzas in relation to the girls. Its application to the murderer transfers its implicit sympathy from them to Matthew Kelly, while in lines two and three, for the first and last time, he is referred to, like Claire and Pearley by his given name only.

Kid Coley forces us to think again about killing. Matthew Kelly, too, has become a victim—of the impersonal killing-ritual of the State.

85

And he faces this with a curious mixture of jauntiness ('his hair combed out in a curl') and heroic irony—for the 'brand new suit of clothes', referred to in his last words, is the clothing the condemned man must wear to the electric chair.

Most songs of this kind are discarded by the singer as time passes, or they die with him. Only chance commercial recording preserved 'Claire and Pearley Blues' and 'The Lawson Family Tragedy'. But sometimes a ballad approaches the archetypal, and then it may become detached from its source in particular events and be performed by many singers—valued for its insight into a recurring human predicament.

This is the case with 'Down on the Banks of the Ohio', for apart from the Ohio River the song is devoid of specific reference—even the protagonists are unnamed. And yet it is this detachment which is, oddly, at the centre of the ballad's power—not only because it could be sung by many singers in many places, but because detachment is relevant to the song's unusual narrative stance. The Blue Sky Boys recorded it in the late 1930s, and it is their version which is followed here.

'Down on the Banks of the Ohio' begins innocuously enough with the narrator addressing his beloved:

> Come my love, let's take a walk,
> Just a little ways away,
> While we walk along we'll talk,
> Talk about our wedding day.

The stanza is trite and seems to be leading into a conventional love story. In fact, as they walk, the lover proposes:

> Only say that you'll be mine,
> And in our home we'll happy be,
> Down beside where the waters flow,
> Down on the banks of the Ohio.

An attentive listener may find it strange that while in the first verse the lover talks as if their wedding day is settled, in the second he makes a proposal of marriage which sounds like a plea—'Only say that you'll be mine . . .' But noticing this hardly prepares us for the third stanza:

> I drew my knife across her throat,
> And to my breast she gently pressed,
> 'Oh please, oh please, don't murder me,
> For I'm unprepared to die, you see.'

Only at this point does it become clear that the lover, and hence the narrator, is deranged. And we perceive this not so much because of the unexpected ferocity of the knife drawn across the girl's throat, but becauase of the shift in tense and in the narrator's relation to the girl. In the first two stanzas she is addressed directly in the present tense and we eavesdrop on their one-sided coversation. But in the third, he has switched to the past tense and the girl becomes third person 'she'. At the critical moment of the murder, we suddenly realize that the action has only been present tense in the mind of the narrator as he goes over his actions in memory. He changes to the past tense when he comes to the killing, however, because it is the one moment which he dare not release into the remembered 'present'. There is an eerie absence of feeling as he goes on:

> I taken her by her lily-white hand,
> I led her down and bade her stand,
> There I plunged her in to drown,
> And watched her as she floated down.

The girl's actions are passive through fear; the man's are numb. He goes back home ''tween twelve and one' (the exactness of timing that of a police report—or of someone who cannot feel); and as he goes he thinks about what he has done:

> I murdered a girl I love, you see,
> Because she would not marry me.

There is a logic to this, but it is the logic of insanity, and it cuts across the lover's perception of time once more, so that we listen as he reverts to the magical 'present' tense:

> Only say that you'll be mine,
> And in our home we'll happy be,
> Down beside where the waters flow,
> Down on the banks of the Ohio.

The repetition floats, isolated, in the afterworld of the deed. In the world outside the narrator's head, however, time passes, the body is found, and next day as he returns home he is arrested by the sheriff with the words: 'Young man, come with me and go/Down on the banks of the Ohio.'

The lover gives no indication of reaction to the sheriff's presence: the sheriff was not there 'standing in the door' yesterday; he is there now. It is as if he cannot react to the real present. But the mention of the Ohio where he drowned all possibility of future, triggers again the continuous present that exists in his mind:

> Only say that you'll be mine,
> And in our home we'll happy be . . .

The song ends at this point without further comment—we have never escaped from the locked mind of the insane killer. But as at the end of 'Claire and Pearley Blues', our understanding of murder and brutality has been extended in powerful ways. Most English-speakers will be unfamiliar with such songs, however, because they are not part of our mass culture, that overwhelms us with words, yet leaves us inarticulate.

Recently, a young girl was stabbed to death in England while she listened to a Walkman. Police said that because of this she would not have been aware of her killer as he approached from behind. Unprepared to die, the girl lay and bled to death. When her body was found the Walkman was still playing—songs of her favourite pop star, Madonna. The irony that she met her death in the self-referring dream world of Madonna was not picked up in the press reports I read. It would have made the perfect subject for a ballad.

WOLF

The City and Nature

In his *Descriptio Londiniae* William Fitzstephen describes how to the north of the city in the late twelfth century there were 'fields for pasture, and a delightful plain of meadow land, interspersed with flowing streams, on which stand mills, whose clack is very pleasing to the ear. Close by lies an immense forest, in which are densely wooded thickets, the coverts of game, stag, fallow-deer, boars, and wild bulls,' while arable land produced 'abundant crops' which 'fill the barns of their cultivators with 'Ceres' plenteous sheaf'. Even in the late sixteenth century John Stow could describe the pleasures of richer citizens in hawking and hunting beyond the city walls, while on May-day, earlier in the century, 'every man, except impediment, would walk into the sweet meadows and green woods, there to rejoice their spirits with the beauty and savour of sweet flowers, and with the harmony of birds, praising God in their kind . . .' Stow and Fitzstephen were eulogists, but they make the point that in pre-industrial Britain citizens lived in daily association with the countryside, even within the tight-packed walls of London.

The obverse of this idyll though was fear, the sense carried through generations, of nature as an oppressive force barely held in check and constantly threatening to overwhelm humankind's hold on civilization. In romance, that map of the medieval mind, the knight is immediately plunged into dense forests and trackless wastes when he leaves the court; nature is at its best in the controlled environment of the *hortus conclusus*, the walled garden where lovers roam in a second, man-created Eden. In the world outside, farmers engaged in a relentless struggle with post-lapsarian nature where wide areas were more or less uninhabited. In the early 1330s, an army led by Edward III against the Scots was lost for several days in the border country, saddles and harness rotting in torrential rain, until a man could be found to guide it on.

For centuries it must have seemed as if little would change. Cities overtook monasteries and peripatetic courts as the centres of culture, and became the source of innovation, power and fashion; but, London apart, they remained small, at once walled in from the nature that surrounded them, and interpenetrated by it. Profound change only occurred in the cities that emerged as part of the industrial revolution.

These rarely evolved from the old cathedral cities, but developed in unlikely places unassociated with traditional centres of power. Eighteenth-century Cardiff and Birmingham grew from nothing to engulf surrounding villages which exist now only as the names of suburbs. The real history of the cities where most people live is barely two hundred years old, and the majority of the inhabitants cannot trace their ancestry beyond their grand or at most great grandparents. By 1851 over half the population of Britain lived in industrial cities, and for the first time in the history of man a powerful society existed which was urban at its core.

Individual memory is short, and city life seems natural or at least inevitable to most of us, though set in the context of humankind's 2,000,000-year evolution it is a radical break with the species' past. The consequences of this are hard to assess because we live so close to them. It seems likely though, that one is the urban dweller's increasing alienation from nature. This is due in part to the vast size of industrial cities which, despite the car, makes the countryside physically remote. A more important cause though, is the function of technology in a mass urban environment.

A consumer society depends for its existence on identifying needs and satisfying them and, increasingly, on stimulating needs artificially. This process has quickened in tempo noticeably since the 1960s, due to the development of high technology products in the home, of which the earliest is television. It is also the most important because of its unique relation to the psychology of the individual. For television creates a closed circuit between the perceiving mind and itself which effectively isolates the individual from his immediate environment, yet maintains the illusion of interaction with the figures on the screen. This has a subtly homogenizing effect, for the illusion is that *Dallas* or *Coronation Street*, the News or *That's Life*, is being presented specially for the viewer in the privacy of his or her home. The presenters of quiz shows, announcers and news readers, are particularly adept at the glance into the camera, the meaningful gesture, which give credence to the illusion.

The reality that millions are sitting at home watching the same programmes is, of course, not lost on the viewer who, isolated in front of his own set, nevertheless has the illusion of experience shared, which can be discussed at work next day. This peculiar duality is put to use by the consumer industry in television advertising. For many adverts half-create in the mind the belief that they are making a privileged offer to the individual, while at the same time engendering the fear that to ignore them would leave him out of the swim.

Not only manufactured goods but ideas, feelings and attitudes are purveyed in a similar way. So television creates a substitute reality which undermines the importance of what is perceived through our own senses in the seemingly more limited world about us. It does this while fostering the illusion of shared experience which is really, however, mass experience received in the form of cellular isolation.

The hard sell of video recorders and home computers has strengthened the closed circuit of viewer and screen. In a strange way, too, modern design seeks to simulate the effect of viewing. The sealed off windows of high speed trains isolate the traveller from the passing scenery, which unreals like a film. On the latest ferries to the Continent it takes an effort to find the way to the deck, for the passenger area is designed as a self-contained unit to satisfy all our needs. Most travellers are content to look through the screen-like windows of the cafeteria, or crowd round the video games machines; few make the effort to go out on deck and experience the wind and sea directly.

As a product of urban industrial society, television naturally projects urban values which are instantly broadcast to the remotest rural parts. People discuss *Dallas* in Caithness as well as Cardiff. Differences still exist of course between city and country, but less and less as urban values play a part in rural life, so that increasingly it is possible to talk of the 'city' not merely as a place but as a state of mind which may exist anywhere. This is reinforced by the exodus of those city dwellers who can afford it to the country, either as weekend cottagers or long-distance commuters. The well-kept rural cottage is likely to be a time-machine, hollyhocks, thatch and mellowed stone hiding an interior out of Habitat. The aim is not to adapt to a very different environment but to structure life so that city advantages are enjoyed in a rural setting.

An interesting phenomenon is the great and increasing popularity of television nature programmes. In a civilization increasingly bent on seeing its image projected from a machine, this may seem paradoxical. To a large degree it is simply an aspect of the closed circuit. Beautifully shot film of the Amazon jungle or the Kalahari desert adds to the sum of a viewer's knowledge but not to his perceptions, for the screen safely isolates him from direct sensory experience. Many people know more about the flora and fauna of the New Guinea rain forest than they do about the sparrow pecking on the sill. The technology of film making in fact tends to discourage direct observation, for the camera's superior eye brings into the home nature as micro and macrocosm on a scale quite impossible to the individual, who watches, fascinated, a half hour programme which took many months of patient field work and weeks of editing in a high technology studio to produce. The mere human eye cannot compete with this, and the world that is open to ordinary observation may seem almost a cheat by comparison.

The same is true of rural life as presented on television. In advertisements, especially, the camera is angled to conceal the motorway, housing estate or factory farm, and appropriate natural sound is dubbed over the more usual mechanical noise of the modern countryside. The result is an idyll which, in our overcrowded society, cannot be—a timeless world which isolates the city dweller further from the realities of the world about him, concealing the ways in which the urban mentality has profoundly affected the countryside.

Part of the paradox though is that nature programmes may also reflect a half-conscious dissatisfaction with things as they are. It is not that urban dwellers wish to live like Amazon Indians, but that they wish for a life different in many respects from the one they have. Films about 'primitive' tribal communities represent touchstones of possibility, while a series like Richard Attenborough's *Life on Earth* affirms the inter-connectedness of all life on Earth which is denied by the closed circuit of urban civilization.

The interesting question for the future is how far such perceptions and dissatisfactions can be transformed by the mass of the people into action in order to redress the balance of our lives, when at the same time we all depend on a high technology civilization which, ironically, provides the medium for the perception in the first place.

In *Trends of Life*, published in the early 1950s, the zoologist F. Wood Jones suggested that Western man, so successful at producing domesticated varieties of other animals, has in the past hundred years undergone a rapid and spectacular process of domestication himself. Domestication breeds dependence, fulfilling many of an animal's functions artificially which it would have to satisfy in the wild by the exertion of its own intelligence. Released into the natural habitat of its ancestors, a domesticated animal either reverts to the wild type as in the case of the pig, or it is eliminated—the likely fate of many of the highly specialized varieties bred today. 'What man fails to realise,' Wood Jones argues, 'is the fact that, under conditions that he euphemistically terms modern Western civilization, he has subjected himself to all the influences that domestication exerts upon other animals. It is impossible to discuss the status of modern man, or to make even a guess at his possible future, unless we bear constantly in mind the fact that we are dealing with a domesticated animal. Man's only distinction from other domesticated animals is that his mating is not, in modern social conditions, habitually controlled by outside agencies.'

The distinction is an important one, as Wood Jones would admit. Yet in the thirty years since he published his book, there is little in our proliferating high technology and increasingly specialized society to contradict what he writes. There is of course no question of going back, of reverting to some ideal type of humankind living in harmony with nature in a predominantly rural society—the dream of some of the urban middle class, who withdraw to become bio-dynamic small-holders, or to run a whole food store. Our civilization has far too complex a hold on the individual for that. The great problem is how to live with the fact of cities and the urban mentality—domestication, in Wood Jones's term—without it leading to a civilization so divorced from the reality of nature that it destroys the environment of the Earth, on which we and all life depend.

*   *   *

In the eight-century Anglo-Saxon poem *Beowulf*, the hall of King Hrothgar is both the factual embodiment and the symbol of an earlier civilization's tenuous hold on a hostile environment. At night its light glimmers through a dark world ruled by monsters. While technology was stagnant, or progressed only slowly, fear of nature that was beyond reasonable control was, as I suggested earlier, a constant in Western man's psychology.

The establishment of Christianity in early medieval Europe fed into this fear in complex ways. The Neo-Platonic element in Christian thought encouraged the division of soul and body to the detriment of the latter, and this merged with Old Testament belief that nature, in its post-lapsarian phase, is fundamentally hostile to humankind. God's curse on Adam rang bitterly true for many a farmer in the Middle Ages:

> . . . cursed is the ground for thy sake; in sorrow shalt thou eat of it all
> the days of thy life; Thorns also and thistles shall it bring forth to

thee; and thou shalt eat the herb of the field; In the sweat of thy face
shalt thou eat bread, till thou return to the ground; for out of it wast
thou taken: for dust thou art, and unto dust shalt thou return.

(Genesis 3: 17-19)

Yet if a hostile environment was part of God's curse on mankind, an
earlier verse in Genesis—referring to before the Fall, admittedly—
placed man in a very different relation to nature. When he created
male and female, 'God blessed them, and God said unto them, Be
fruitful, and multiply, and replenish the earth, and subdue it: and
have dominion over the fish of the sea, and over the fowl of the air, and
over every living thing that moveth upon the earth' (1: 28). Whether
or not, in theological terms, man's lordship over the creatures of Earth
was revoked at the Fall, the idea was a powerful one which sanctioned
an innate human assumption about our species' superior worth, and
the rights which accrue to us on that count.

In the pre-industrial West a limited science and technology circumscribed man's lordship, though the idea of *use*—that the Earth exists to
be subdued by man as a right—fuelled Renaissance explorers, con-
querors and their heirs, as it did early industrialists. Natural ambition
and greed were no doubt the prime motives, but divine sanction was a
powerful weapon to use against self-doubt or the questioning of
others. Developments in chemistry, physics and related technologies
in the nineteenth century opened up a Pandora's box of possibility,
however, and while the growth of science was paralleled by the slow
decline of religion, the idea of use, of dominion over nature, remained
as a first principle of the new era. It seemed as if man's lordship might
at last be transformed into reality and that through our understanding
of science we might revoke, unilaterally, as it were, 'God's curse'.

It now seems that although scientists have learnt a lot about the
Earth, they have not learnt enough, and that our commitment to sub-
duing the Earth, rather than living with it, is having an accumulat-
ively destructive effect on the environment. This is mainly so because
human-induced change, at an ever increasing pace, is out of phase
with our own development as human, that is biological, beings.

In *Nature, Mother of Invention*, Felix R. Paturi makes a distinction
between *development* and *design*. By development he means the slow
evolutionary process in nature which produces forms adapted to their
environment. Design is the technologist's simulacrum of this process
—the testing and rejection of hundreds of thousands of permutations
to arrive at the best design for a product. Superficially design seems to

96

follow the principle of natural selection; in fact, as Felix Paturi demonstrates, there is a fundamental difference. Developments in nature, occurring over a long period of time, are in phase with the environment: 'They will not outstrip it and therefore force it to adapt itself to them.'

Designs, on the other hand, can be produced at an ever quickening pace, as scientific knowledge and technological expertise increase by geometrical progression. In such conditions:

> . . . the machine does not belong to the environment of *natural* man; rather, natural man belongs to the *biological* environment of the *artificial* machine. The dilemma of our time consists in man having to adapt himself to the machine, because its maturing principle, which is design, advances more rapidly than the maturing principle of man, which is development. Hence the progress of the machine may prove fatal for man. And since he himself is the design engineer, he is committing suicide.

More people in the West are becoming aware of this, of course, though they remain a minority. Why this should be so poses interesting questions about *natural* man, to use Felix Paturi's term. For if we are on the verge of an ecological crisis, why aren't the governments of the developed nations taking radical action? And why aren't the majority more concerned? There are a number of answers. In the first place we are confronted by a situation which is unique in the history of humankind: there are no precedents to Western man's complex industrial civilization. Consequently there is no way of knowing for certain the long term effects of the industrial processes and machines we have come to consider indispensable to our way of life. It is not surprising therefore that scientists cannot agree, for example, about the possible influence of carbon dioxide on the atmosphere. The 'greenhouse effect' is something *extrapolated* from known data about the environment, supplemented by what is known of the atmosphere on Venus. It is only something which *may* happen, and the calculations involved are so complex that the same evidence can be used to predict quite different results. Under these conditions the scientist is reduced to a latter-day haruspex, and governments and individuals are free to consult whichever pleases best or suits their needs.

It is here that the psychology of *natural* man may be a crucial factor in the fate of the Earth. On a geological time scale, human design-induced change is taking place with unprecedented speed. This is equally true in human terms if we consider the species' 2,000,000-year biological development. However, the major negative changes that are or may be taking place are barely visible in the span of one lifetime, and our inbuilt sense of time—human time—cannot cope adequately with this. We respond immediately to a disaster that is before our eyes, like the famine in Ethiopia and the southern Sahara, but hardly at all to the potentially catastrophic effect of carbon dioxide in the atmosphere. Almost everyone wants a car and can give good short term reasons for possessing one. How many give more than a passing thought to carbon pollution which may produce devastating effects hundreds of years in the future? We live by a kind of natural selfishness which in a balanced ecology is presumably necessary to survival, but which, in one that is out of balance, resembles the image of the much-maligned lemmings, rushing blindly to a cliff and disaster.

Moreover, in the West, the species' natural selfishness is utilized in a way which compounds the problem, returning us to the closed circuit of city mentality. If a domesticated animal, like a dog, is given unlimited food, it eats to excess—an atavistic instinct, presumably, in response to conditions in the wild where the food supply is irregular and uncertain. The human species responds in a similar way to plenty, and this has been harnessed by the consumer society to its own ends. Advertisements stimulate desire, appealing to short term gratification, which industry proceeds to satisfy. The complex edifice of our civilization depends on this and it is accepted openly or tacitly by the majority. Government, too, is involved. Long term planning means thinking five, ten or fifteen years ahead to ensure that there are sufficient natural and energy resources available to feed industry. Industry itself thinks only of short term gain, and, together with the mass of the populace, which has come to depend on immediate gratification as its *raison d'être*, comprises a powerful lobby against radical restructuring of society. Only when immediate interests are threatened in ways that are palpable will government act against industry, or industry attempt to restore a natural balance it has itself destroyed. Thus the decimation of European softwood forests by acid rain is likely to lead to concerted action, while the dumping of nuclear waste at sea is not.

Short term measures against specific environmental problems may give the impression that things are more or less under control—that science and technology can right any imbalance that science and technology have created. But this is a false perspective engendered by the human time scale on which we tend to project our hopes for the future. Minor imbalances in the environment may be checked after they have occurred. But if chemical pollution results in overheating of the atmosphere, and a greenhouse effect in one or two hundred years, we will have produced a situation beyond human control. The problem we face is the need to change our lives radically *now* in order to avert what is only a possible (some would say probable) disaster many years after we are dead. It seems doubtful if *natural* man is capable of thinking in such terms, especially under the conditions of domestication we have created for ourselves in the urban environment.

For the closed circuit of city mentality, which encourages us to live in the moment, increasingly makes us indifferent to the future as it has made us indifferent to the past. This in itself reflects profound changes in our attitude to lineal descent. I mentioned the fact that most people in industrial cities cannot trace their ancestry beyond their grand or great grandparents—a function of the way in which the first industrial generations were displaced from settled communities rooted in place. In a society such as ours, governed by rapid change and the need for mobility, direct family ties are rarely maintained beyond a generation or so and even less for collateral branches.

In a less mobile rural community, families are bound by patterns of land tenure, associations with place and by simple geographical proximity. In such a society the individual is in part identified by his ancestors, for, so the thought goes, to know a man's forebears is to know the man. It is equally important to plan ahead as far as possible for future generations, by husbanding the land and its resources as a familial, hereditable unit. The society of medieval Iceland, for example, was deeply influenced by such ideas, which are a dominant force in the sagas.

In industrial society, the individual will feel concern for the future of his or her children and grandchildren, but it is hard to think beyond, for even grandchildren are likely to be scattered and have little direct contact with their grandparents. In a consumer society the land no longer acts as a link between generations. We have substituted cash, goods and, maybe, a house—all of which are freely negotiable items. A child rarely grows up to live in the same house as his parents, let alone his grandparents. If he inherits it, it will be sold, for he lives elsewhere and has lost all but the most tenuous connections with the area where he grew up. A house is a valuable inheritance but only in so far as it can be converted into capital, that prerequisite of a mobile society. Capital, however, is impersonal, passing with the same value from one individual to another in the market place. It cannot have the

same kind of familiar associations that bind a family through generations. There is no longer a sense of the Earth (in terms of a family's
hold on one small plot of it) as a heritable place held in trust. Disinherited from a familial past, we are thus in a direct sense disinherited from
the Earth. So, instead of improving on a pattern of land use which,
despite its many inadequacies, was based on conservation with future
generations in mind, we have felt ourselves free to substitute rapid
exploitation, banking on technology and the chemical industry to
right any imbalances that may occur.

Anyone who tries to confront environmental issues may experience
a sense of paralysis. The situation is so complex, and the forces ranged
against radical change are so overwhelming. Indeed, it is probably
impossible for the individual to understand what is happending in any
comprehensive way. Even if he is an expert, it is likely to be in a small
field, and the problems of environmental pollution are at once global
and interactive. Under these conditions a priority must be to break, by
whatever means, the closed circuit of city mentality. For unless we can
be persuaded to change the values and assumptions by which we live,
and to do so radically, it is hard not to see a bleak future for the Earth
and the life it supports. A beginning would be to counteract the
increasing specialization fostered by our education system as it
focusses ever more narrowly on the needs of technology and business.
This does not mean producing 'generalists', but men and women who
are capable of seeing their expertise in a wider scientific and humanist
tradition. There is need for a civilized and civilizing education system.
But trends in Western education are against this and toward the
grossest kind of utilitarianism, dedicated to the servicing of the closed
circuit.

Fault Lines

In 1987, conservationist Marion Shoard published a book called *This Land Is Our Land*,[1] the cover of which is illustrated by a heraldic 'achievement', the shield being quartered: dexter, a combine-harvester advancing on ripened wheat; two game birds (a ptarmigan close, a pheasant volant): sinister, a stile, rustic and beflowered; a red admiral splayed. On a compartment of turf are the 'supporters': dexter, a sportsman, armed, capped and plus-foured; sinister, a booted hiker, levi'd, with rucksack and binoculars. Each grasps a garter which encircles the shield and bears the legend 'The Struggle for Britain's Countryside'. Together with the title—a snatch from one of Woody Guthrie's more sentimental songs—the achievement gives a fair idea of Marion Shoard's subject. For despite its length (nearly 600 pages) and its wealth of factual detail, the argument of *This Land Is Our Land* is essentially simple: during the early Middle Ages the land was stolen from the people of Britain and remains even now in the hands of a small minority which exploits it for profit and pleasure. In fact, according to Marion Shoard, through its social and political influence, by adopting intensive farming methods and by investing in lucrative government-backed conifer afforestation, this group has more than maintained its power-base and has handsomely increased its profits.

But the cost, as she amply demonstrates, has been the widespread destruction of the traditional British landscape and the decimation of our fauna and flora. At the same time, the mass of the people, crowded in towns and cities, have been barred from access to the vast tracts of beautiful countryside in private hands—countryside which ought to be everyone's birthright. Landowners, she argues, must be made to give up some of what they consider their 'rights' in land in order to conserve the countryside and its wildlife, and to share its beauty with others through increased right of public access. Why we find ourselves in this situation and what can be done about it are Marion Shoard's themes.

Some of the facts she collected in writing this book are interesting. In 1986, for example, 87 per cent of land in the United Kingdom was

[1] Paladin, pb.

101

in private hands and there is evidence that the percentage will increase. The Forestry Commission, which held 2,878,785 acres in 1986, expects to sell about 10 per cent of its holdings by 1989 at an estimated profit of £1,000,000. Who owns the current 87 per cent? According to Marion Shoard, the popular notion that financial institutions like insurance companies are moving into land is false. About 80 per cent is still privately owned, much of it, of course, by farmers, and many of them small farmers. But one third of the 80 per cent is in the hands of aristocratic families, with 200 families owning more than 5,000 acres each in 1967. Marion Shoard says there is no reason to believe things have changed in the intervening years. In fact, far from being crippled by death duties—a popular belief exploited by the landowning aristocracy—this group, together with the gentry, has succeeded in conserving its landed wealth by adopting new management methods and by hiving off much of the land into family-owned limited companies. So, large parts of an estate may not, on paper, appear to be 'owned' personally at all, though the head of the family will be the head of the company, or its majority shareholder, thus ensuring *de facto* control. Land managed in this way is big business and profitable. In 1976, the richest one per cent of our citizens owned 52 per cent of all land in private hands.

Most of this land is either intensively farmed, afforestated with conifers, or kept like so much of upland Scotland as preserve for game. Since it is privately owned, the public is barred from almost all of it. More surprisingly, out of one and a half million acres of so-called common land in Wales and England, at least 1.2 million acres are enclosed, with the result that 'ordinary citizens enjoy no legal right to roam and can be treated as trespassers'.

The current system of land ownership in Britain is clearly unacceptable and in need of reform, and it is Marion Shoard's intention to explore the means of achieving this. Ironically, however, this intention is the cause of a fundamental weakness in *This Land Is Our Land*, for the book is written to a programme which leads her to introduce historical and ecological data in support of her argument when convenient—but to distort or ignore them when they might seem to contradict her preconceived conclusions.

To take the historical background first, since it provides essential underpinning of her argument. Land tenure in Anglo-Saxon England is described under the sub-heading 'Saxon Innocence'. Here she states correctly that during the early period, after the Anglo-Saxon

conquest, land was almost certainly in the hands of independent peasant farmers, the ceorls, who held directly from the kings. But what is
Saxon innocence? It is never quite defined, though Marion Shoard's
exposition of land tenure in the period makes it clear that it was the
absence of an intervening landed aristocracy; the fact that the land was
held independently by those who cultivated it. However, it is also well
known that 'The institution of slavery was part of the earliest English
law, and in view of later evidence there can be no doubt that the primitive English ceorl was usually a slave owner'.[2] Marion Shoard recognizes this but in terms that are rather disconcerting: '. . . even at this
early stage [i.e. during the conquest and settlement of the fifth and
sixth centuries] a certain amount of perversion of the system was
already taking place. Supporting what seems a relatively innocent
form of family-subsistence agriculture was a class of slaves—probably
Britons who had been expropriated when the Saxons conquered their
country.' Writing of the ninth and tenth centuries, the French
agrarian historian Georges Duby points out that 'At that period the
whole of Western Europe practised slavery, and probably nowhere
more actively than on the less advanced fringes closer to pagan lands,
such as England and Germany.'[3] Slavery was not a development of
this later period, the snake in the Edenic garden of independent
peasant farmers. It was the inheritance of Roman civilization and of
the early Germanic societies. Slavery was inherent in the socio-econ-
omic system the Angles, Saxon and Jutes brought with them to these
islands.

However, ceorls working the land in independent family-sized
units come close to the form of tenure Marion Shoard considers desir-
able. The fact that the ceorls of the early period gained their land by
conquest and farmed it with the aid of slaves is therefore muddied over
with vague phrases such as 'a certain amount of perversion' and talk of
'relative' innocence—terms which distort history as well as raise
serious questions of ethics.

The confusion of thought evident here deepens as Marion Shoard
traces the history of land tenure through the Middle Ages. 'The
[Norman] Conquest,' we are told, 'eliminated the early Saxon notion
of land *ownership* by working farmers. What took its place was a form of
ownership by conquest.' There are two things to be said about this.
One is that for some time before 1066 a number of thegns had amassed

[2] F.M. Stenton, *Anglo-Saxon England* (OUP, 1971).
[3] *Rural Economy and Country Life in the Medieval West*, (Arnold, 1968).

103

large estates which in themselves clearly undermined the principle of ownership by those who actually worked the land. The second is that land held independently by ceorls in the sixth century was also a form of ownership by conquest—conquest of the Romano-British. One man's freedom is another man's conquest. It is at least arbitrary to make ethical distinctions in an historical context between two equally thoroughgoing conquests, each of which depended on a form of slavery at its social and economic base.

Muddled thinking also vitiates her account of the transition from a feudal to a capitalist agrarian economy. 'Feudalism had allowed little scope for the individual serf to improve his position. One of the advantages of capitalism was that it allowed the hard-working peasant blessed with good luck to produce food for the market as well as for his own family. In so doing he stood a chance of eventually being able to enlarge his own holding by buying out other peasants.'

Marion Shoard is very far from being a supporter of capitalism, but this statement is extraordinary; for with its reference to the 'hard-working peasant' who gets on with the help of the unidentified blessing of 'good luck', she echoes capitalist apologists who see those who do not prosper as shiftless good-for-nothings. And who are the people this new kulak class was buying out? The shiftless? Or those whom the new agrarian economy deliberately pushed to the wall? What she is really saying is that under early capitalist conditions, some peasants were able to better themselves by joining the ranks, at the lowest level, of the capitalist entrepreneurs through the exploitation of their fellows. What improvement is that?

So much is admitted by Marion Shoard herself in the next paragraph, but in such a way as to contrast early capitalist agriculture with a paternalistic feudalism which 'at least guaranteed the livelihood of large numbers of people by providing them with employment and enabling them to grow their own food on land which the lord was expected to provide for them'.

But this is to romanticize feudal society and indeed to contradict her own earlier account of it. Peasants may have made some marginal gains during the agrarian crisis and social unrest following the bubonic plague of the mid-fourteenth century; but the late medieval aristocracy and gentry nonetheless saw land as a source of wealth to sustain the conspicuous consumption and display which were the visible symbols of their social status. Likewise the early capitalists—

and their followers—bought into land not only for its potential in exploitable wealth, but because of its potential for exploitable status.

This is explicitly denied by Marion Shoard when she says that the gentry of the sixteenth century who made their fortunes in the professions, in royal service or as merchants, lacked the older aristocracy's sense of land as 'a trust to be exercised on behalf of the sovereign' and instead 'regarded their tenants and lands as things to be exploited automatically, whereas for the established landlords this attitude required something of a rethink'.

Marion Shoard confuses feudal ideology with late feudal practice here; at the same time perpetuating the myth of an 'old' aristocracy which was in essence different from the parvenus who sought to emulate it, if not to join its ranks. In fact, there were few genuinely old aristocratic families in England in the late Middle Ages. 'Only three comital families in 1400 had enjoyed their dignity for more than a century: Vere, Beachamp and Fitzalen. The rest of the earldoms in 1400, namely fourteen, were creations of the previous seventy-five years; well over half, ten out of the total of seventeen, of the last fifty years. As a group the earls in 1400 were mostly newcomers to their rank. And in this . . . 1400 was in no way exceptional. The higher ranks of the nobility rarely deserve the epithet "old". The turnover was always rapid, the eminence short-lived, the survivors invariably few.'[4]

The intense concern of the late medieval aristocracy with wealth derived from land, together with the fact of the high extinction rate among aristocratic families, are largely ignored at this point in the book—because Marion Shoard's aim in the historical survey is to point up an ever decreasing sense of responsibility on the part of owners in relation to the land and its people, from the archetypal ceorl, though a late feudal 'paternalist' aristocracy, to exploitative capitalism. But her account reveals the same mix of over-simplified history and muddied ethics that we have met before. Two hundred pages later, when discussing entrepreneurs who bought into land in West Newcastle in the nineteenth century, she makes the point—equally valid for the fifteenth and sixteenth centuries—that buying into land brought with it at least the hope of greater social prestige for the upwardly mobile *nouveaux riches*, who were as eager to adopt 'aristocratic' values as they were to exploit land for its potential wealth.

[4] K.B. McFarlane, *The Nobility of Later Medieval England*, (OUP, 1973).

When she turns to the modern period, her argument fractures along other, and from a contemporary viewpoint, more important fault lines. Marion Shoard notes that intensive farming methods have, since the 1950s, led to widespread destruction of hedges, ponds and marginal land in the name of an efficient agriculture: that is, larger field units, increased use of pesticides, herbicides and chemical fertilizers, and the factory farming of animals—and all done with no concern at all for the beauty of the landscape or the life forms it sustains.

However, she presents this as if it were something quite new, a process whereby 'Farming as Britain had known it for generations gave way to a relentless process of industrialization.' Yet even her own historical survey shows that post-war trends are only the latest in a process of agricultural development by 'improving' landowners who since at least the sixteenth century have been draining wetlands, felling deciduous forests and destroying wildlife in the pursuit of profit. The ecological effects are more severe now because they are more intensive, but loss of species, for example, is nothing new in Britain. 'Up to the end of the eighteenth century the great bustard nested in wild places in England and south-west Scotland and the "droves" which roamed over the Yorkshire wolds, Salisbury Plain and similar uncultivated areas were often immense, but the bird was too big and edible to survive.' 'The history of the hoopoe as a British bird is a long, disgraceful obituary.' 'The too conspicuous avocet is indeed almost a "lost British bird", for a century ago it nested in some numbers in the eastern counties from the Humber southward.' These are the observations of T.A. Coward in *The Birds of the British Isles*. As he notes, the invention of the breach-loading gun was a major factor in the decline of many species in the nineteenth century; but the crane, a common species in the Middle Ages, last bred here according to ornithologist James Fisher about 350 years ago, and disappeared despite Tudor legislation designed to protect it. Destruction of habitat was almost certainly a major factor.

Many species were hunted to extinction by the aristocracy, gentry and gentleman-farmers for sport or as 'vermin'. But they are not the only people who enjoy killing, as Marion Shoard would have the reader believe. The stalking of deer and riding to hounds may be the prerogative of the country rich, but there are many others who enjoy hunting and baiting badgers—or shooting small birds with air rifles. Marion Shoard is unwilling to admit this, however. There is only one villain in this book, and that is the landowner. One strand of her argument says that the destruction he is causing to the countryside must stop; the other, that the land must be opened up to the public, 'For the numbers who seek inspiration from the countryside to refresh their daily lives run into many millions.'

Here she creates for herself a problem. Even if the destruction could be halted—and perhaps parts of Britain reinstated as upland moor or wetland—would increased pressure on the land for recreational purposes have a damaging effect on the environment? Marion Shoard is adamant that it would not:

> In very heavily used spots, even resistant species are unable to survive the trampling they receive and the bare ground that is exposed may be eroded by wind and rain. But this is a small problem. Very, very little countryside is actually trampled away. The threat to landscape or wildlife caused by public recreation is just not a sufficient reason for keeping people out.

Yet the evidence she uses to support this assertion is flimsy and, to say the least, selective. She quotes, for example, from an interview she conducted with Colin Stubbs, the Nature Conservancy Council's assistant regional officer in Hampshire. There has been a loss of species in the New Forest, but is this due to increased recreational use by the public? Colin Stubbs' answer is equivocal: 'It is perfectly true that around parking and camping sites the land has become trampled and worn; there is also the secondary impact of tree felling around car parks. Locally this is having an effect and if you multiply it up it is significant.' What does this mean? Either increased recreational use is having an impact on the ecology of the New Forest or it is not. Colin Stubbs seems to imply that it is, but then he denies it, conveniently for Marion Shoard, in the sentence that follows: 'However, no species changes in the forest can be attributed to recreation. The wildlife population changes that have taken place have been due to quite different factors, like over-grazing. From an ecological point of view, the problem of over-grazing is far greater than recreation.' What then is the 'effect' locally, due to increased recreation, which Colin Stubbs at first says is 'significant' if you 'multiply it up'? He does not say and Marion Shoard does not ask.

To take one other example she refers to an experiment conducted by the British Field Sports Society to see how far pheasants might be disturbed by the presence of people in woods where they breed. The 'experiment' is what you might expect from the British Field Sports Society. It consisted of sending in a pack of fox hounds and hunt horses, thrashing about, barking and tally-hoing through several woods. Next day, a check was made on the pheasant population. Numbers seemed constant: there was no evidence that they had been disturbed. From this Marion Shoard engineers the conclusion that increased public access to such woods would not affect game birds like the pheasant, nor other species of wildlife. It appears from her account, however, that the 'experiment' was made only once in each wood. This is completely unacceptable as evidence that larger numbers of people roaming in a wood, on a regular basis, over several years, would have no discernible effect on wildlife. Had Marion Shoard spoken with a wider range of naturalists and ecologists she would have received very different answers. Answers, however, which do not support her thesis. The evidence is therefore never presented.

I talked with Graham Burton, information officer in Wales for the Royal Society for the Protection of Birds. He told me how increased recreational use of beaches and sand dunes in the past fifty years has had a severe adverse effect on the population of ringed plovers and little terns; how more and more walkers in upland areas are disturbing rare raptors like the hen harrier and the merlin; and how the galloping of horses on the mudflats of the Wirral are frightening off the thousands of waders that winter there and for whom the flats are essential feeding grounds.

Some people employed in countryside management in west Wales are concerned at the erosion of fragile cliff-face plant communities along the Gower and Pembrokeshire coasts by rock climbers, who may also pose a threat to rare birds like the chough and peregrine falcon during the breeding season—though research into the latter is at present insufficient. Even those who might be expected to take a responsible attitude are sometimes involved in the destruction of sensitive habitats. In some west Wales locations, botanists have so trampled certain sites by kneeling to photograph rare plants that they have ended by destroying the plants.

This leads to another distortion in Marion Shoard's argument. She consistently represents the typical outdoor recreationist as the informed, concerned hiker, the painter, photographer, or family picnicker. Such people are essential to her argument that the countryside should be opened up to people in their 'many millions'. But while such people exist, they are not the only, or even the most typical 'users' of the countryside. Marion Shoard never mentions the power boats and water skiers who make, for example, Llangorse Lake in Powys a noisy hell in summer, nor the hang glider clubs whose members swoop off the scarp slopes of the Black Mountains in Gwent, disturbing buzzards and kestrels from their hunting grounds, nor the cross-country motorcyclists, the whine and snarl of whose engines can be heard for miles across the hills, and whose bikes tear up the grass tracks which are already seriously eroded by those other apparently harmless recreationists, pony-trekkers. Nor does she mention the micro-light aeroplanes whose pilots, according to Graham Burton of the RSPB, are causing serious concern by buzzing tern colonies.

I talked with Tudur Wynn-Jones who farms 420 acres on Pen Llŷn. He is one of a small number of conservation-minded farmers, who has planted deciduous copses on his land, created a pond which has become a habitat for wild duck, and who keeps his traditional stone walls in good condition. In recent years, however, he has become frustrated and disillusioned. With the increase in tourism in Pen Llŷn in the 1980s, he has had stone walls broken down by hikers crossing his land at arbitrary points, despite existing footpaths, as well as cases of people deliberately pulling them down. Vandals have also uprooted oak saplings he has planted. His sheep have been worried by tourists' dogs on the upland pasture. He finds that bird watchers tend to be responsible: they ask permission and he gives them free access to his land. Tudur Wynn-Jones identifies tourism as the main source of vandalism on his farm. In his opinion, increased public access would have a deleterious effect on the areas he has set aside for wildlife.

Marion Shoard would, in the first place, deny that vandalism was an important factor in the countryside generally or in the disturbance of wildlife. Secondly, she would argue that opening up the millions of acres that are in private hands would spread the burden of recreation over a wider area. Graham Burton of the RSPB is also in favour of open access to wild places if they are properly managed. He is, however, in favour of zoning of the kind that exists in the Snowdonia National Park, where people are encouraged to go to certain areas where there are picnic facilities, etc., while more sensitive wilder areas are open to those who want to go there, without being actively promoted or encouraged.

This is anathema to Marion Shoard—the herding of people into countryside ghettos. But the RSPB information officer believed that such zoning is essential in environmentally sensitive areas. While increased access to private land would be good because it would indeed ease the pressure of numbers on other areas, nevertheless he insisted that a significant increase in visitors in any particular area would have a negative impact on species.

Marion Shoard's ideal, far from zoning, is the *Allemansrätt* (lit. Everyman's Right) of Sweden, which gives all Swedes 'the right to cross another person's land on foot providing no damage or disturbance is caused'. She admits that Sweden 'has a smaller population' than Britain, and that 'much of it is remote forest', but argues that *Allemansrätten* works equally well in the heavily populated south as in the remote north. As presented in *This Land Is Our Land*, a form of *Allemansträtten* sounds an attractive solution to the highly restrictive access to private land in Britain. But the analogy is false, for Marion Shoard misses out essential data. Although noting that the population of Sweden is 'small', she does not mention that it is in fact just over 8 million, nor that the land mass of Sweden is 449,792 sq. km.. The United Kingdom has a land mass of 244,755 sq. km. and a population of just under 56 million. In other words, the entire population of Sweden is about 1 million more than the population of London, but it has almost twice the UK land mass to wander in. Turn these statistics around and, in Britain, we have seven times the population of Sweden crowded into just over half the land mass.

The fact is, the British Isles are hopelessly overcrowded and any increased access to the countryside by people in their 'many millions', to use Marion Shoard's phrase, is going to have a damaging impact on the natural environment and on wildlife species—no matter how much land is opened up.

There is one other fundamental difference between Sweden and, at least, England, which Marion Shoard neglects to mention. Sweden must be the most highly socialized nation in Europe if not on Earth. To an outsider, this may sometimes make it seem like an extremely conformist and in some ways oppressive society; but one of its positive sides is that most Swedes are highly conscious of their social obligations. This is not the case in the 'selfish society' which increasingly characterizes the fragmented, urbanized environment of Britain. *Allemansrätten* works in Sweden because the overwhelming majority of Swedes are responsible, and because their population is small relative to the country's size. It would not work in Britain not only because there are too many people crowded into too small a land mass, but because too many of them are ignorant of or indifferent to the problems confronting the countryside. It would be unthinkable in Sweden to find the rubbish—Coke cans, crisp packets, plastic beer bottles—that litters the hedgerows, the hills and shores of Wales; or to find people, as Tudur Wynn-Jones has done, deliberately pulling down the field walls on his farm. And his is not an isolated example. Farmers and landowners who ruthlessly exploit the land for profit are major factors in the decline of the countryside, but so are the tourists who pollute and in some cases destroy the natural beauty they purport to wish to see.

All of this is omitted or dismissed by Marion Shoard because it does not suit her programme. She dismisses 'The brief environmental panic of the 1960s' which led to the creation of country parks and picnic sites in an attempt to control the mass exodus from the cities each summer. She claims that by the mid 1970s 'it was clear that the simple equation of numbers of visitors with pressure on the country-side was mistaken', that the birth rate had fallen in the late 1960s and that 'car ownership projections based on the assumptions of endless growth looked much less convincing once the recession of 1973 had begun to bite'. She then quotes Derek Barber, chairman of the Countryside Commission, who told her in 1982 that he put conser-vation before increased public access. Marion Shoard comments: 'In sacrificing the opening up of the countryside, Derek Barber was very much in step with the conventional wisdom of 1968.'

Since 1982 it would seem that Derek Barber and the Commission have re-thought their position. In *Enjoying the Countryside: Priorities for Action* and *Policies for Enjoying the Countryside*, two policy documents published in 1987 in connection with its 'Recreation 2000' programme, the Commission outlines its plans to increase public use of the countryside. This includes better signposting of public rights of way, increased rights of access through co-operation with farmers, rangers to help and advise visitors, and the education of citizens in their rights of access. In all of this there is much talk of the conservation of 'attractive countryside', accompanied by the inevitable photo-graphs of clean-cut, rucksacked hikers and responsible-looking pic-nickers—but very little mention of any possible impact on wildlife.

Yet despite Marion Shoard and the new-look Countryside Com-mission, it is impossible to have it both ways. Millions of people roam-ing the countryside by the year 2000 will mean no more hen harriers or merlins, fewer and fewer plovers and terns. Typically, the change in land use which is bound to come in many areas, because of agricultural over-production within the EEC, is seized on by 'Recreation 2000':

> This could lead to greater priority for public recreation which, instead of being seen as a threat, could not only become part of the rationale for conserving the countryside but also offer some limited opportunities of alternative income to those who live and work on the land. Meanwhile, many jobs in tourism depend on the attractiveness of the countryside and the services which tourists help to sustain also benefit those who live there.

These could be the words of Marion Shoard (and in fact 'Recreation 2000' echoes many of her proposals) or of the Wales Tourist Board. It is the new 'conventional wisdom' of public bodies, and a certain kind of conservationist, with professional interests in the restructuring of the countryside that is likely to take place in areas such as Wales. 'Conservation' is one of the key words here, but always in the context of human *use*. The underlying idea of *This Land Is Our Land* is still, in essence, that of the private landowners: the Earth is here, as by a kind of natural right, to be used by the human species. In Marion Shoard's case, and in that of the Countryside Commission, use is related to the pleasure of the greatest possible number instead of the privileged few.

The animal rights movement is seen by most as an extreme and unbalanced fringe in our society; yet in some ways a profounder ethic underlies its perception of our relation to nature than Marion Shoard's. Any idea of rights, of natural law, is of course an arbitrary concept of the human mind unless, as a Christian, you anchor it in some rather dubious statements in Genesis. It is the imposition of an ethical ideal on the natural processes of the Earth which act quite outside the boundaries of any such concepts.

There is, however, no logic in limiting the concept of 'natural rights' to our own species. Why should the hen harrier and the red kite not have a natural right to broad areas of moorland, largely devoid of human beings, which they need for hunting and breeding? Moreover, doesn't the human mind itself need such areas: the *idea* of an upland moor, quartered by a harrier, the idea of an estuary mudflat feeding thousands of waders, where no human ever approaches? Such areas seem to me essential to the human imagination in these overcrowded islands. It is the idea of nature without, so far as is possible, human disturbance.

112

Last year I met a man who believed this too. Somehow we got around to discussing it, and he told me that he had never mentioned it to anyone before because he knew most people would think he was mad.

The Laureate and the Firm

The appointment of Ted Hughes as Poet Laureate in 1984 caught literary journalists off guard. Philip Larkin was everyone's choice until rumour spread that he had refused the post before it was offered. After that several poets in the second rank were canvassed, though without much enthusiasm. For reasons that seemed self-evident at the time, Ted Hughes was thought by most to be out of the running. When the name of the new Poet Laureate was announced, therefore, journalists reached for their clichés in a desperate attempt to find copy. 'The Earthy Poet Laureate' was *The Financial Times'* response next morning. ' "True Poet" Ted Hughes is Laureate' wrote *The Times* rather limply. 'The Poetic Voice of Blood and Guts' said *The Guardian*. Two days later, *The Times* tried again: 'The Crow Man as Tribal Poet'.

There was a sense of unease mixed with vexation in the reports. For his piece in *The Guardian*, John Ezard had the good idea of phoning round members of the English literary establishment for their predictably negative responses. Philip Larkin, he learned, had been 'the only name recommended by the Arts Council for forwarding by Downing Street's patronage secretary to the Queen'. 'It's deplorable,' Geoffrey Grigson told him. 'He's such a bad poet. He can't write. I'd sooner have had Larkin any day. Larkin has much more dignity.' The latter's friend, Kingsley Amis, put on his best Garrick Club manner: 'Dog doesn't eat dog, but it's a bit thick. One was gradually getting used to the idea of having a bishop called Jim Stepney—and now we find ourselves with a Poet Laureate called Ted Hughes.' 'Hughes is a good poet,' conceded John Medlin, publications officer of the Poetry Society, but then he added: 'It will be interesting to see whether he makes himself into more of a public figure and public ceremonial poet —or whether he simply goes on churning out nature poetry.'

The snide dismissal of Ted Hughes's poetry in that last remark found an echo in several of the press reports. David Holloway, for example, acknowledged in *The Daily Telegraph* that 'If the intention is that the Queen should give the poet laureateship to the best available poet, then Ted Hughes is a good choice.' What he gave with his right hand, however, he took away with his left. 'But should it be intended that the Poet Laureate would produce suitable verse for royal occas-

114

ions, then Mr Hughes is not the man. His rough rhymes and harsh imagery would be uncomfortable for describing, say, a royal christening.' For the rest, Holloway damned with faint praise and assented with civil leer. 'However, as our leading nature poet, he might find some sort of inspiration from the wild life of Balmoral.' 'There is no doubt that Mr Hughes is a fine poet, even if some of his images ("my breath left tortuous statues in the iron air") are extravagant and his technique, at times, suspect.' 'With him the laureateship could never be said to be in safe hands but whatever he gives us is unlikely to be dull, obsequious or even technically correct.'

Metropolitan critics have always distrusted Ted Hughes. His poetry is rooted in the rhythms of Middle English alliterative verse with its stubborn provincial base in West Midlands and Northern dialects. It is the polar opposite of the fashionable neo-Augustanism of the capital. It is also founded on belief in the primacy of our relationship to nature at a time when most would sooner forget it. For this reason it has seemed easy to dismiss him as a 'nature' poet, as if his verse is a menagerie of animals and birds. In fact, Ted Hughes is a religious poet whose religion is based on a pre-Christian celebration of nature. This finds expression in many of the poems on the this-ness of the lives of birds and animals, but there is also a substantial body of mythic verse such as *Crow, Gaudete, Cave Birds*, 'Adam and the Sacred Nine' and 'Prometheus on His Crag'. As with all religious poetry there is a level where these poems demand assent of a non-literary kind. This is deprecated by urban and urbane critics in England who tend to prefer the distancing irony, elegance and wit of the 'Martian' poets, who, lacking conviction themselves, makes no assault on the reader's.

No wonder there was perturbation in Fleet Street in November, 1984. But if members of the literary establishment were hard put to understand how he came to be appointed Poet Laureate, it is not difficult to see why Ted Hughes himself found the offer attractive. The answer is there in one of his first public utterances after his appointment—'The Crown is the symbol of the spiritual unity of the tribe. When that's outmoded, so will be the Poet Laureate.'

Interestingly, Philip Larkin had said something very similar in a *Paris Review* interview two years earlier. Asked about the laureateship, he replied: 'Poetry and sovereignty are very primitive things. I like to think of their being united in this way, in England.' But he was uncertain about the Laureate's function: '. . . it's not clear what the Laureate is, or does . . . it isn't a job, there are no duties, no salary, and yet it isn't quite an honour, either, or not just an honour.' And he took the opportunity of laying the grounds for his own refusal should the office ever be offered to him: '. . . the publicity that anything to do with the Palace gets these days is so fierce, it must be really more of an ordeal than an honour.'

As a sidelight on the muddied history of the appointment, it is worth noting that Kingsley Amis is quoted in *The Guardian* on 20 December, 1984, as saying of Larkin: 'I am absolutely sure he was going to be asked. He also told me several times that he would turn it down.' Yet in an article in *The Guardian* on 8 December 1986, Noel Hughes, another friend, claims that Philip Larkin had told him in 1971: 'I want to be Poet Laureate. I want it very badly indeed.' There is no reason to doubt either friend's statement. Noel Hughes had advised Larkin that if he wanted the post he should increase his output and be less retiring. After *High Windows* (1974), however, he dried up as a poet. When Sir John Betjeman died, Philip Larkin had not published a collection of poems in ten years. It is reasonable to assume that this, together with his intensely private nature, made him realise that acceptance was impossible.

Whatever the truth here, Philip Larkin's comments in the *Paris Review* reflect a general uncertainty about the function of what is widely seen as an antiquated public office. Ted Hughes, characteristically, wrenched the laureateship in the direction of his own concerns in a statement about the Crown which was framed as a dogma and a challenge. This was picked up by *The Times* in a more or less sympathetic leader on 22 November. (Conservative papers like *The Times* and *The Sunday Times* were noticeably more favourable to Ted Hughes's appointment.)

> He is an atavistic poet, insistently fixing his attention on the violence at the roots of nature, and effortfully carving out home-made myths about God and Crow, resembling chopped-up mixtures of the *Niebelungenlied* and the *Just So* stories. It is a style further from modern everyday life, with its infinitely various and touching detail, than the subject-matter of Betjeman and Larkin . . . But of course there is something atavistic about the idea of royalty, too. Mr Hughes showed his awareness of that by remarking in his first interview that the Crown was 'a symbol of the unity of the tribe'. He may, unusually among modern laureates, be one for whom the idea of being a tribal poet may prove a powerful stimulus to the imagination.

116

At a glance Ted Hughes's statement seems straightforward but, in fact, it is difficult to understand. In what sense, for instance, can the population of Britain, in its millions, be said to constitute a tribe? When the word *spirit*, like *soul*, has been emptied of meaning by our rationalist civilization, what meaning does it have for Ted Hughes? What does 'spiritual unity' mean? And how is the Crown a symbol of that unity?

The answers are to be sought, at least, in Ted Hughes's character-istically mythopoeic vision of life. He does not merely exploit myth for literary purposes, as *The Times* leader suggests. Rather he believes that certain myths are manifestations of a real power in the Earth and that our psychological or, as he would say, spiritual health depends on our recognition of that fact. This power is represented in some of his mythic poems as a female principle or goddess, the central deity of a pre-Christian nature worship which was repressed, though not destroyed, by Christianity, and which survived in attenuated form in the figure of Natura, Dame Nature, in Medieval and Renaissance theology and art. In some of Ted Hughes's poems this female princi-ple seems to be used as a symbol; in others, however, there is no doubt that it is intended—in some sense—literally. This is to cross the divide between poetry which makes use of myth as story or allegory and poetry of religious conviction. Some of Ted Hughes's poems are not meant as stories but as revelations.

Such belief, like all religious belief, is not open to rational proof, but it does not matter in this connection whether Ted Hughes's nature rel-igion is true or not. It is sufficient that he himself believes it to be true and believes that the problems of Western civilization in the twentieth century are the direct result of a failure to incorporate its truth into our lives. The 'Note' that follows his *Choice of Shakespeare's Verse* is illumin-ating in this respect.

Because he *is* a religious poet, one function of Ted Hughes's mythic poetry, from *Crow* on, has been to embody powerful symbols of trans-formation. He is not, in fact, the bleak poet metropolitan critics say he is. The nihilistic Philip Larkin is far bleaker. Moreover, because his poetry reflects, in his view, the process whereby the powers of nature work themselves out through our lives—whether we admit this to ourselves or not—he is equally on the alert for symbolic events and acts of transformation in society itself. It is highly likely that this influ-enced his acceptance of the post of Poet Laureate, a post which must have been especially attractive to him because the reigning monarch is a queen.

This is made clear in one of his most ambitious occasional poems to date, 'The Crown of the Kingdom', published on 21 April 1986, and subtitled 'A Celebratory Pageant for the Sixtieth Birthday of Her Majesty Queen Elizabeth II'. It is a long poem in which the Queen is the unseen centre of a pageant which plays out some of Ted Hughes's deepest convictions. Seen from the point of view of the Establishment, it must make him the most subversive Poet Laureate ever.

Ted Hughes's opposition to Christianity is a matter of record in poems like *Crow* and in published interviews. He sees its orientation towards the male principle in the figure of God, and its dualist elevation of the spirit at the expense of the material world to be at the root of our troubles. In this poem, Christianity is subtly paralleled and parodied.

Three 'Angels' are central to 'The Crown of the Kingdom', but they are Angels of Water, Earth and Blood, rather than the ethereal creatures of Christian tradition. They bear gifts as an act of homage to the Queen: the first brings water, a recurrent symbol of transformation in Ted Hughes's recent poetry. This water, cupped in the Angel's hands, is a mirror in which 'the one face of the millions . . . Bends to sip the wholeness'. The second is a 'care-worn Angel. An old midwife crone' who is the principle of Earth itself, bringing her gift of 'the goodness of earth'. The third bears blood, which is the unconscious linking of heredity,

> Single
> As the tangled, crimson, twisted yarn
> Of lineage and language.

The bearing of gifts, the symbolic use of water and blood, the sacred figure 3, point obliquely to Christian tradition, and Ted Hughes clearly means the reader to perceive this. But his symbols are grounded in pre-Christian religion and the poem as a whole is profoundly anti-Christian. The Angel of Water has polluted modern streams in its veins, and its pores are wells, pagan cult centres and shrines—'blocked wells, lost wells' which are, ironically, 'marked with a cross'. The gifts of the Angels are overtly contrasted with the gifts of the Magi at Christ's nativity. The Angel of Earth does not bear frankinsense or myrrh or spermicetti 'in her mountainous hands', but something 'brighter than blinding snow'—which is 'the goodness of earth'

> (As from the Islands' every corner
> As for Adam.)

There is a fine irony in Queen Elizabeth II, Defender of the Faith, being presented by her own Poet Laureate with a poem in which she is the votive centre of a pre-Christian nature religion. Side-pieces, as it were to the main pageant, present the weaving of a floral crown for the Queen, and thirty birds of the air bearing sixty birthday candles—birds who 'looking for God, find a Queen', who is cast in an unmistakeable rôle as the human representative of the goddess of nature.

The centrepiece of the pageant, however, is the forging of the 'Crown' out of the mixed races, the overlapping conquests and assimilations which have gone into the making of 'Britain'. There is a further irony in this because although Ted Hughes's aim is undoubtedly to subvert the Establishment view of the monarchy, this central section of the poem falls back on an interpretation of English history which could have come from the pen of Alfred Lord Tennyson. We are given a potted history of these islands: Neolithic and Bronze Age men are followed by 'the tread of the Legions' and the 'Wolf-headed' Anglo-Saxons who 'Breed from whimpering girls/Howling berserks'. Then Vikings 'inched the longships/Under Holderness' and so on. The Celts are present too, making their contribution to the forging of the 'nation':

> And here is the harp that came on the air
> As a fairy bride
> Murmuring Gaelic—
> That set its chords
> In place of the bars
> In the dungeons of English.

This is Form One history of two generations ago. As a tableau in a pageant it is reminiscent of emblematic paintings from the high period of Victorian imperial power: the Great White Queen sitting in state while representatives of her subject peoples, the kilted Scot, the half-naked black, kneel in homage, offering up tributary gifts symbolic of the far-flung Empire.

Even stylistically, Ted Hughes has fallen back on the clichés of imperial laureate verse: 'the tread of the Legions', 'mercenary brothers', 'Howling berserks', 'inched the longships' would not be

119

out of place in a poem by Alfred Austin. It is un-Hughesian, dead, compared with this quick-sketch of a pansy from an earlier section of the poem:

A Pansy, little pug-face,
Baby Panda—
(An intricate, masterly Japanese brush-stroke
Dabbed her identity signature)

'The Crown of the Kingdom' helps make clear what Ted Hughes meant by that first statement as Poet Laureate. It is the mass of the people, the millions linked through heredity, through the folds and layers of history who are the tribe, whose association with these islands constitutes the immutable bond of the nation with the land; while the Queen, whose crown is forged from that people, is symbolic of its spiritual unity by virtue of her sacral rôle in a nature religion which survives in some sense despite ourselves.

There is, however, an extraordinary disjunction between this version of the Queen and the one presented to us daily by the press and on television. There is little doubt that in early Anglo-Saxon society kingship had a sacral rôle of the kind invoked by Ted Hughes,[1] but centuries of Christianity and the constitutional struggles of the late Middle Ages and Reformation destroyed its last vestiges. In this century the monarchy has recognized that to maintain itself it must accommodate to the times. It is not surprising, therefore, in a post-war society which is obsessed with the economy and expresses worth in terms of the market value of a product to find that the current Royal Family, according to the popular press, refers to itself jokingly as 'The Firm'. Nor in an age of democratic levelling, media hype and the cult of 'personality' that The Firm has promoted itself as a family radiating niceness and decency and social concern. They could almost live next door, at least in the more affluent suburbs.

At the same time, the Royal Family are 'stars' and while we are meant to feel close to them, they are nonetheless infinitely distanced. We relish the sense of familiarity while responding to the glamour of their apartness: 'The machinery of mass promotion encourages this identification by simultaneously exalting and humanizing the Olympians, endowing them with the same appetites and eccentricities that we recognize in our neighbours.'[2] Anyone who has followed *The*

[1] See, for example, William A. Chaney, *The Cult of Kingship in Anglo-Saxon England* (Manchester University Press, 1970).
[2] Christopher Lasch, *The Culture of Narcissism* (1979; Sphere Books, 1985).

Daily Mail's obsessive coverage of the Royal Family's 'domestic life', will have noticed this.

There is a similar ambivalence in the antiquated ceremony that surrounds the Queen on State occasions and her involvement with the hard sell abroad of British industry. Echoes of an imperial past are used as a backdrop to the promotion of high technology. In this light, a more appropriate tutelary deity for the monarch than Nature would be Mercurius, protector of traders.

Ted Hughes might reply that his perceptions of the Queen may nonetheless be true, despite the media promotion of her and The Firm with its mix of meretricious glitter and domestic decency. At a sub-conscious level the tribe, or those millions who read the popular press and watch television, may be responding to deeper needs, symbolized by the Queen in her disguised sacral rôle—needs expressed by Ted Hughes thirty years ago in the poem 'Boom':

> More More More
> Meaning Air Water Life
> Cry the mouths
>
> That are filling with burning ashes.

But whatever one thinks of this kind of mythopoeic view of society, it is a fact that Ted Hughes's laureate verse has not, so far, been very good. The occasional poems he has published have either been written to a programme, like 'The Crown of the Kingdom', or they have been simply bad. His 'Song' for the marriage of the Duke and Duchess of York, for example, reads as if he had been possessed by the poetic spirit of the previous Laureate, Sir John Betjeman:

> A helicopter snatched you up,
> The pilot it was me.
> The props, like a roulette wheel,
> Stopped at felicity.

This contrasts markedly with his most recent collection, *Flowers and Insects*, which confirms his stature as a major poet. His failure to date as a writer of laureate verse is almost certainly due to his investment of a decayed institution, the monarchy, with a significance it cannot bear. Nonetheless, the continued attempt of the Poet Laureate to transmute the titular head of the Church of England into his version of the Queen of the May is going to be interesting.

121

Heroic Laughter

Mention the hero today and the muscle-bound Rambo is likely to come to mind—the 'hero' of pulp fiction and videos who always wins out in a killing-game with enemies of an inferior race. The heroic as a concept to be taken seriously seems moribund if not actually dead. Yet ordinary people can still be touched by the heroic in its older and profounder sense and can admire, for example, the captain in the Falklands War who died in a reckless one-man attack on a machine-gun nest. This is disapproved of by liberal intellectuals as a distasteful vestige of an earlier militarism. Few stop to consider that perhaps those who admired the captain were responding to something deeply rooted in human nature. Certainly few poets would chance their reputation by writing a heroic poem about such a man. It might nonetheless be worth taking a closer look at that unfashionable concept, the heroic, and what it means.

Strange as it may seem, laughter is an important feature of heroic literature. In *Y Gododdin*, Eithinyn who rushes into battle, and his death, is described as a 'spear-thrusting lord, laughing in combat'. That laughter echoes three centuries later in the Anglo-Saxon *Battle of Maldon*. Byrhtnoth, leader of the Anglo-Saxon host, spears a young enemy warrior in his neck, then pierces another through his chainmail so that 'the deadly point was fixed in his heart'.

> The earl was the gladder,
> the brave man laughed   gave thanks to God
> for the day's work   which the Lord had given him.

Shortly after, Byrhtnoth himself is killed.

That is one pole of the laughter of heroes, when the battle-heat is up. The other is expressed in Chaucer's *Troilus and Criseyde*. Troilus, undeceived at last as to Criseyde's faithfulness, takes revenge on the Greeks in battle where 'thousandes his hondes maden deye' until he is cut down by Achilles. At his death, his soul is carried up to the eighth sphere, from which great height he looks down at 'This litel spot of erthe, that with the se/Embraced is'. Finally, his eyes fall on the plain of Troy where he was killed:

> And in himself he lough right at the wo
> Of hem that wepten for his deth so faste;

And dampned al oure werk that foloweth so
The blynde lust, the which that may nat laste,
And sholden al oure herte on heven caste.

These may seem, merely, two contraries—a warrior code celebrating the deeds of an earthly hero, and a Christian ethic which condemns any such heroism as vanity, 'blynde lust'. In fact the positions are not so far apart. The warrior code of the Celts and Anglo-Saxons had engrained in it knowledge that our lives are brief and often futile; a knowledge which was reinforced by Christianity. But the warrior code survived conversion in many ways intact, and had, in turn, a profound effect on the perception of Jesus in early medieval Europe. Nowhere is this more clearly seen than in the eighth-century Anglo-Saxon poem *The Dream of the Rood*, a monologue in which the Cross, personified, narrates the story of the Crucifixion and its significance for mankind.

Since the fifteenth century, we have become so used to the image of the suffering of Christ in art that it can be something of a shock to contemplate the Christ Triumphant of early Celtic and Anglo-Saxon crucifixes. So in *The Dream of the Rood* the Cross describes how at Golgotha

I saw the Lord of mankind
hasten with eager zeal   since he wished to mount me.

Jesus, at the point of being crucified, is described as *'geong haeleth . . . strang and stithmod'* (a young hero . . . strong and courageous). He *'gestah'* (ascended) the Cross, *'modig on manigra gesyhthe'* (brave in the sight of many). While at the climactic moment, the Cross trembled *'tha me se beorn ymbclypte'* (when the warrior clasped me).

This description, though qualified by clauses such as 'he who was God Almighty' and 'since he wished to redeem mankind'—which attempt to place Jesus in a special category—is nonetheless equally applicable to the heroes of *Y Gododdin*, to Byrhtnoth and Beowulf. Interestingly, the purely human sufferings of Jesus on the Cross, which were to be made so much of by fifteenth-century pietism, are, in *The Dream of the Rood*, largely transferred to the Cross itself, leaving Jesus freer to fulfil the rôle of triumphant hero—'They drove *me* through [says the Cross] with dark nails . . .'

This may seem a far cry from the Jesus of the Bible—the superimposition, in fact, of a warrior code on a religious leader of a very different stamp. Yet the Gospel narratives must have made the interpretation easy, for they contain many motifs common to heroic literature, and it is not going too far to suggest that—within a complex and amibiguous context—the Gospels themselves presented Jesus in the rôle of hero. In fact, the post fifteenth-century view of him as passive sufferer of betrayal, torture and death fits less easily with the Gospel account than the heroic Jesus of *The Dream of the Rood* who not only participates in, but eagerly embraces his death.

Among many parallels with heroic literature, there is the gathering of the Apostles, a chosen band who are asked to take on great odds; while nonetheless it is the hero in the end who is singled out by fate, and by his superior prowess, to accomplish the deed, and whose greatest moment of triumph is his death.

Most significant, though, is precisely that razor edge between will and fate which identifies the hero. If his actions are unequivocally the result of one or the other, then he is the victim of his own pride, or of an irrevocable destiny. In either case he is no hero. The heroic consists in that mix of the two in a proportion which is indeterminate and indefinable, yet which it is important for the reader to perceive as there. When Gunnarr Hamundarson, one of the heroes of *Brennu-Njáls Saga*, is unjustly exiled from Iceland for manslaughter, he appears to accept his fate. But as he rides off from the family farm

> . . . Gunnarr's horse stumbled, and he had to leap from the saddle. He happened to glance up towards his home and the slopes of Hilíth arendi.
> 'How lovely the slopes are,' he said, 'more lovely than they have ever seemed to me before, golden cornfields and new-mown hay. I am going back home, and will not go away.'

In *Gísla Saga*, Vesteinn is returning from abroad to stay with his friend Gísli. But Thorkell, Gísli's brother, is plotting to kill Vesteinn for adultery with his wife. Gísli dispatches messengers to warn him off, and sends with them a half-coin which will match one in Vesteinn's possession. Long ago, the friends had agreed only to send the half-coin in a great emergency. The messengers miss Vesteinn's party, however, until he is well on his way. When they catch up with him

> . . . they hand over the coin which Gísli has sent him. He takes out the other half of the coin from his money belt and turns very red as he looks at it.
> 'You speak the truth,' he says, 'and I should have turned back if you had met me sooner, but now the streams all run towards Dýra-fjord and I shall ride there; and in any case I want to go. The Nor-

wegians [in his party] will turn back. But you get on by boat,' says
Vestennin, 'and tell Gísli and my sister of my coming.'

They go home and tell Gísli. He answers: 'That is how it must be,
then.'

In the first example, fate takes a part in Gunnarr's life when his
horse accidentally stumbles. Without this, he would not have looked
back at the homestead, but rode on into exile. His glance at the beauty
of the fields, however, leads the hero to a decision: he will not leave. It
is a decision which he and the reader know must lead to his death.

In *Gísla Saga*, the mix is slightly more complex. Through a series of
unfortunate mischances, Gísli's messengers fail to catch up with Vesteinn until he has reached a watershed on the moors. Pride is mixed in
Vesteinn's motivation, though in what proportion it is impossible to
say. It is clear, though, as described by the saga writer, that the watershed is psychological as well as geographical. There are moments in
life when you can't turn back, in honour, even though you see clearly
the consequences. Prudence, and self-preservation at all costs, are not
heroic virtues. The sweep of the streams down towards Dýrafjord is as
inevitable as a fate which Vesteinn not merely accepts, but like Christ
in *The Dream of the Rood*, positively embraces.

It is this clear-sightedness which is—or in pre-modern times was
thought to be—one of the hero's most admirable traits: for Vesteinn
and Gunnarr are not entirely passive victims of fate; rather, they ride
fate like a wave, through an act of will, knowing it will lead them to
their deaths.

In the events leading to his crucifixion, Jesus exhibits precisely
these features. He sees as clearly as Vesteinn what will happen to him.
As tells the Apostles:

> Behold we go up to Jerusalem; and the Son of Man shall be delivered
> unto the chief priests, and unto the scribes; and they shall condemn
> him to death, and deliver him to the Gentiles.
> And they shall mock him, and shall scourge him, and shall spit
> upon him, and shall kill him: and the third day he shall rise again.
>
> (Mark 10. 33-34)

The narrative technique is very different from that of the sagas, in
that Jesus makes explicit what will happen to him—though he is
curiously distanced from events by the use of the third person 'he'.
Anyone familiar with the understated mode of saga narrative will
know that Gunnarr and Vesteinn foresee their fates just as clearly.
Everything is implied by Gísli's 'That is how it must be, then.'

125

In Mark's Gospel, Jesus now sets about an extraordinary course of action in which he provokes fate and yet, as it were, averts his eyes from it. His violent behaviour in the temple, when he 'cast out them that sold and bought . . . and overthrew the tables of the money-changers, and the seats of them that sold doves', seems designed to goad the authorities into taking action against him. Yet when asked by the chief priests and the elders, 'By what authority doest thou these things?' he takes refuge in the tricky subtlty of the saga or folk hero:

> . . . I will ask of you [he says] one question, and answer me, and I will tell you by what authority I do these things.
>
> The baptism of John, was *it* from heaven, or of men? answer me.
>
> And they reasoned with themselves, saying, If we shall say, From Heaven; he will say, Why then did ye not believe him?
>
> But if we shall say, Of men; they feared the people: for all *men* counted John, that he was a prophet indeed.
>
> And they answered and said unto Jesus, We cannot tell. And Jesus answering saith unto them, Neither do I tell you by what authority I do these things. (Mark 11: 29-33)

At this point Jesus has accepted his fate; embraced, like the saga heroes, the wave that sweeps him to his death. Yet, like Gunnarr and Vesteinn, he will only provoke events so far—after that, fate, in this case in the form of the temple authorities, must act upon him. It is most important in heroic literature, however, that even when fate, in the form of an accident, takes a hand or seems to take control, the hero is seen to make a choice: Gunnarr could have remounted his horse; Vesteinn could have returned to his ship; Jesus could have turned aside from Jerusalem. But once the decision has been made—the leaning with rather than against fate—then a curious passivity often overtakes the hero, and his ultimate end is imposed on him by others.

In heroic battle poetry, the process might seem different, but in practice it is very similar. In *The Battle of Maldon*, once Byrhtnoth has made the decision to allow the invading Danes to cross the causeway with their superior numbers, the outcome of the battle is inevitable. Once the heroes of *Y Gododdin* have set out, there is no turning back from death against hopeless odds.

At a crucial moment, though, the life of Jesus deviates from that of the hero—the moment of his death. St Mark's Gospel describes how

> . . . at the ninth hour Jesus cried with a loud voice, saying, Eloi, Eloi, lama sabachthani? which is, being interpreted, My God, my God, why hast thou forsaken me? (15: 34)

126

Jesus's cry, recorded in the earliest Gospel and echoed by Matthew, suddenly places him in a different category from the heroic, for it can only be interpreted, surely, as a cry of despair, an acknowledgement of some inner sense of defeat—after which, according to Mark, he cries out loud once more, then dies. The rending of the temple veil is a narrative touch which adds to the solemnity of his passing but, however Jesus's words are interpreted, they are hardly heroic. The hero, once set on his course to death, dies silently or, as in some of the Icelandic sagas, with an ironic or caustic comment on his lips. After a certain point a decision has been made; words are useless.

When Jesus cries out, he abandons the rôle of hero and forces us back onto the ambivalence of the ordinary, the human. That is why his life is fascinating even to non-Christians. For he was either a hero who failed, or a god—who by definition could never have been a hero, since the heroic is essentially a human possibility in which the hero goes to his death against the odds, in a vain cause, and with full knowledge.

Seen from the heroic perspective, therefore, Jesus fails the last test, in a sense the only test, of a hero—his death. When heroic literature describes a hero's death, it is meant to be admired. The death of Jesus invokes pity, fear and uncertainty, but it seems to avoid, almost deliberately, admiration. In the death of a hero, there are no surprises: he is what we knew him to be all along. But if Jesus was divine, or thought he was, then narratorially his last-minute deviation from the heroic at precisely that moment when the life of a hero should have been fulfilled, was essential.

Contemplation of Jesus's death must leave the Christian with a bewildering array of feelings which arise from what seems, almost, a botched death, a betrayal. At the moment when his followers expect a sign of hope, they are given a suffering man. Yet it is, ironically, precisely the suffering of this equivocal god-man which creates the means by which the Christian finds his own faith. To fulfill *that* rôle— of Saviour—Jesus had to stand back, in the end, from the heroic stance which had, apparently, borne him so far.

Today the heroic is not much considered. Even the word has been debased to a synonym for 'brave'. But while bravery is an essential part of the heroic code, it is only a part, inextricably combined with personal and social values, some of which are unpalatable today. The personal especially perhaps—the hero's aggressive preoccupation with honour and pride, and the ultimate obsession of heroic societies with death. We, too, are obsessed with death but in a way which cancels out the heroic. As I suggested, for the hero, how he dies is the ultimate validation of how he lived. Life in the early Middle Ages was short and the vanity of vanities motif of biblical tradition blended well with Welsh and Anglo-Saxon experience in the heroic age. The laughter of Troilus which mocks the futility of purely human endeavour was readily internalized.

But yet, the hero snatched, or thought he could, something of worth from our brief lives—validating the human by adhering to what was in many ways an ascetic code which prepared him to face death unflinchingly. For this complex of reasons, the hero often appears to embrace death eagerly, or at least to lean into the current which he knows will sweep him towards it.

It is this lack of fear of death in the hero which we find hard to accept. For in our society the aspiration of many is to live to be ninety-nine and die surreptitiously on mind-dimming drugs in our beds. This is the opposite pole to the heroic code which held that you should see clearly to the end.

Moreover, even in a largely non-Christian society, Christian perceptions have remained lodged in our culture—not the Christianity of the heroic age, but the humanistic piety of the fifteenth century and after, when it became the fashion to emphasise the suffering of Jesus. Nowadays we have transposed that to ourselves: our central Western view of mankind is one of suffering and pain—which we wish to avoid ourselves and alleviate in others, though not at the expense of our own standard of living.

There seems no room for the heroic, with its insistence that a short life lived well is better than a long one brought to a feeble end. Nor do we approve of the aggressive assertion of will which often leads the hero to his death regardless, apparently, of its consequences for others. In the twentieth century, the ideal fighter has become, not the hero who breaks ranks to gain undying glory for himself in death, but the *guerillero*, the ambusher, who hits and runs to fight again.

Yet when the genuinely heroic does burst in upon our society, it does so with a shock which is combined, for many, with a bemused fascination and even admiration. Whoever has seen war-film footage of the Polish cavalry charge against Nazi German tanks, during the invasion of Poland in the Second World War, can never forget it. There you had an elite, trained in the last vestiges of the heroic tradition, it is true. For them, there was no option: the slope down which they charged was their watershed.

When an individual outside the tradition takes on the heroic it is more surprising, and suggests, perhaps, that there is something in the psychology of some people which responds in a particular way to changes in body chemistry at moments of intensity near death, or when the individual perceives that he may be near death. In the one car crash I have experienced, our driver crossed a T-junction into on-coming traffic. It could not have lasted more than two or three seconds, yet as the leading car crashed into the side of ours, I had a sensation of riding a curve and that everything had slowed down to fit this one, perfect curve. Then we crashed, glass spattered over my back, and as logic and panic took over, we got out of the car as quickly as we could.

I think that curve is in some way at the centre of the heroic code, which through its rigorous ethic, showed selected men how to 'ride' it open-eyed to their death. The curve is no doubt a function of adrenalin in the brain at moments of great stress, but it also relates to what used to be called fate. In life, so the thought went, you can ride the curving wave of your fate willingly or, as most of us try to do, duck under it.

In a non-heroic society, no one knows how he will react in such extremes, for action of this sort is not part of our ethos, we are not pre-pared for it. Yet there are instances of behaviour so close to the heroic code that it suggests the code itself is rooted in a certain kind of human need which asserts that the measure of our life is our death.

Denmark is a placid country with a tradition of neutrality and pacif-ism in our century. The 'Viking' spirit has long been dead as a social ideal. This partly explains why the Germans were able to hold it so easily in the Second World War: Denmark was 'occupied' rather than conquered, and given 'favoured nation' status by the Nazis. There was, nonetheless, a small resistance movement from the beginning which was in itself more courageous for being disapproved of by a large if indeterminate section of the population. One of the move-ment's leaders was Jørgen Schmidt, who came from a middle class family in the comfortable Copenhagen suburb of Hellerup.

After several years underground, the Gestapo finally tracked Jørgen Schmidt to a villa where he was recuperating from wounds. His death is recounted by John Oram Thomas in *The Giant Killers*, a history of the resistance movement in Denmark. As the woman he was staying with was being questioned by Gestapo officers at the door,

Schmidt shot one of them from the top of the stairs. Panic followed, the Gestapo called in troops and the villa was surrounded. Jørgen Schmidt kept them at bay, however, through the night until the house began to burn down around him. Finally, according to an eye-witness, the roof caved in and the walls started to collapse:

> Then, suddenly, he charged through the smashed French windows, a wild, slight figure in blood-soaked blue-and-white pyjamas. He rushed out onto the lawn, the Sten-gun at his hip still firing.
>
> He got only a few steps before they cut him down. He looked like a pathetic doll crumpled on the grass.
>
> But he went out as he would have wished—fighting to the last.

This account of a modern instance is very interesting. Jørgen Schmidt's end is reminiscent of a saga hero's death, at bay in a farmstead in Iceland. But the eye-witness, a modern Dane, far removed from such events, has no adequate language with which to describe what he has seen. His first reaction on seeing the body of the dead man is to emphasise the pathetic—it is 'like a pathetic doll crumpled on the grass'. That is, his first reaction draws attention to externals—what we might say after witnessing a traffic accident. No doubt the corpses of the warriors at Catracth would have looked just as pathetic seen through the lens of a news camera.

The eye-witness realizes that this is not enough, however—Jørgen Schmidt was a hero in the traditional sense and he, the eye-witness, has seen something rare in our society. But the heroic is an inner experience. The poets of the heroic age don't describe the pathetic mangled corpses, the objective (from our point of view) scene of a battlefield, but the inner workings of the hero's mind, the scene viewed with his stylized vision. The anonymous eye-witness to Jørgen Schmidt's death dimly perceives this but has no adequate words to express his perception. He falls back on cliché—'he went out as he would have wished—fighting to the last'. That is the end-line of a B-Western or gangster film, the shadow-play of the heroic tradition.

What to do with the death of a man like Jørgen Schmidt? The heroic is unfashionable, partly because it is misunderstood, but also because the majority of Western poets and intellectuals find it inherently distasteful. Anthony Conran's 'Elegy for the Welsh Dead, in the Falkland Islands, 1982' contrasts the deaths of the Welsh guardsmen in that war with the heroes of Catraeth. It is written out of indignation at the futile deaths of the young soldiers in a war which should never have been fought:

Figment of empire, whore's honour, held them.
Forty-three at Catraeth died for our dregs.

Yet what are we to make of the running comparison of the guards-men's deaths with those of the warriors of Catraeth? Unless I misread the poem, Anthony Conran is suggesting that the warriors' deaths, too, were inherently a waste. As epigraph to his poem, he quotes two lines from *Y Gododdin*:

Gwŷr a aeth Gatraeth oedd ffraeth eu llu;
Glasfedd eu hancwyn, a gwenwyn fu.

Men went to Catraeth, keen was their company.
They were fed on fresh mead, and it proved poison.

Quoted out of context, the emphasis is on 'poison'. The implication is that the year's feasting before that battle was a poison-cup, and Anthony Conran parallels, rather than contrasts, this with the guardsmen who 'feasted' for three weeks in a luxury liner on the way to *their* death.

Placed in context, however, the lines from *Y Gododdin* have a different significance. The warriors may have drunk a bitter drink, but they died heroically, and the poem is a celebration of this as well as an elegy. As in *Y Gododdin*, Anthony Conran names the men who died:

Certainly Tony Jones of Carmarthen was brave.
What did it matter, steel in the heart?
Shrapnel is faithful now. His shroud is frost.

The second line is ambiguous. It could mean 'steel in the heart did not matter, because he was brave'. A more likely meaning in the general context of the poem, however, is: 'what does bravery count for, when all it leads to is an early death'.

The answer of the heroic poet would be that if Tony Jones was brave at his death it did matter. It is possible to take Anthony Conran's position partly because we know, or suspect, that those guardsmen were not trained in, and never thought of themselves as operating within, a heroic code. Were the heroes of Catraeth watching pornographic videos when they died? We no longer value the heroic and so do not prepare for situations where its values might be a factor in human dignity.

Nor, consequently, do we have a poetic which could allow itself to celebrate it. The last heroic poem I know is W.B. Yeats's 'Easter 1916'. Almost all poetry since, which is considered 'acceptable', has

131

followed the line of Wilfred Owen. No wonder Yeats disliked his poems and excluded them from his Oxford anthology.

And perhaps that is it. The genuinely heroic will surface from time to time—to be manipulated by the Right for propaganda purposes, and ignored or disparaged by the Left-leaning intelligentsia. Either way, it is unlikely to be celebrated, or have its true meaning interpreted, by the poets of our time.

Brendan Kenelly's Cromwell

What does history mean to most people? A beach of random facts shelving quickly into deeper and darker waters of myth and legend where a nation shapes its identity. The majority have little concern for the inductive analytical attempt of the historian to understand the past. Instead they home in on the lives and deeds of great men and women, 'great' meaning good, or evil, depending where the doer stands in relation to the national self-image, and on generalizations, half-truths that become *idées-fixes*. 'History' as such is simple, crude, confused. But it is also alive in a way that academic history cannot be and should not be—an organic thing; the past rooted in the dead, but flowering and fruiting in the lives and deeds of the living.

In this sense, Oliver Cromwell must be one of the most emotive and powerful forces at work in Ireland today, and Brendan Kenelly has taken his centrality—his monstrous myth, but also the equally monstrous truth of the Lord Protector's involvement with Ireland—and made it the focus of one of the finest sequences of poems to appear in some years.[1]

The other central character is M.P.G.M. Buffún, a contemporary Irishman, who at the outset of the book, invites Cromwell into his 'emptiness'. From that point, Buffún lives out what Brendan Kennelly sees as the nightmare of inherited Irishness—through a series of voices and guises that move in and out of history, legend and fantasy.

One of the profoundest aspects of *Cromwell* is the perception of how words embody conceptual frameworks which limit and direct our behaviour. Oliver Cromwell has an over-riding sense of destiny, of the rightness of his cause. He expresses this through an imagery which is revealing in ways that he could never understand. He is the surgeon, the healer—'I came here knowing I had surgery to do.' He is the conqueror-as-friend; though, in the Classical tradition of friendship which held that a true friend tells the truth, he is Ireland's 'severest friend'. Underlying any such 'friendship', of course, is the controlling idea of power, which not merely qualifies the proffered friendship but turns it into a threat:

[1] *Cromwell* (Bloodaxe Books, 1987).

133

Write down this in the blank page of your mind,
Cromwell is my friend as England is my friend,
And will be, if I obey, to the end of time.

The threat implicit in the advice is made explicit and fused with concepts of guilt and crime, projected onto the Irish in Cromwell's conclusions:

Ponder these simple, deep, unending words.
Do as each word bids.
Do not, you will be punished for your crime.

Words are part of the weaponry of the conqueror. Here a professed 'friendship' to a 'sick' society will yield just retribution for 'crime', should the conquered not accept the conqueror's terms. In comment, the words have to be put in inverted commas (though not in Cromwell's speech), because this use of language has a double structure: involving the surface meaning of words which are well known, and the underlying structure of meaning they are made to carry, which is quite different—making it necessary to read and 'read' them.

But Cromwell, like the later administrators of the British Empire, is incapable of seeing this disjunction: his mind is closed in a conceptual framework which demonstrates daily that he is an instrument carrying out the Lord's work. The ruthlessness of the Protestant English army under his command, however, prompts an equal cruelty of response from the Irish 'rebels'—the half-hanging, then cutting down, and hanging again, of captured soldiers, Irish girls who slept with them and other collaborators. And the Irish response expresses itself in words, too, in a rhetoric which is the mirror image of the assured, God-directed language of Cromwell. In 'Do Good' a Protestant is dug from his grave and his corpse flung over the graveyard wall. The anonymous speaker of the poem admonishes his compatriots:

The land of Kildare will never be sanctified
Till the last heretic's bones
Are plucked from the clay and destroyed.
They must not escape just because they are dead.
Death brings no pardon to guilty skeletons.
Know this. Then go and do good.

Without the context of the octet of this sonnet, these could be the words of Cromwell. Each side is locked in a rhetoric which justifies, as it dic-

134

tates, atrocity. Each is enmeshed in a language which precludes knowledge of the enormity of what it has done.

Cromwell explores this in the context of Irish history, but underneath is the perception of a truth about humanity itself, enshrined in the Latin proverb *Homo homini lupus est* (Man is to man a wolf). It is a perception which is ironically half perceived (but only half) by the commander of a besieging Irish force who, in an echo of Cromwell's language, refers to the besieged English as 'not human', 'beasts' who

> if they persist as beasts
> I'll answer by hanging, drowning in rivers,
> Ditches and holes . . .

Humanity founders on such rhetoric which is not recognized as rhetoric. In 'Oliver Speaks to his Countrymen', he begins: 'I have no rhetoric, no wit, no words,' which is itself a rhetorical commonplace. It is followed by what is, given its premise, an irrefutable logic:

> The Dispensations of God upon me
> Require I speak not words, but things.

'Things' is ambiguous. It could mean deeds—actions speak louder than words. But it also clearly means concepts—the concept of the Spaniard as the enemy of God, of the 'Being of England'. And concepts lead us back to words. What Cromwell and his enemies cannot see is that they are enmeshed in a structure of perception where 'words' are confounded with 'things' which have, at best, a questionable reality outside the words which enshrine them. Cromwell believes that 'things' release him into truth, into reality—whereas in fact they strip him of his humanity.

But then what is this humanity which Christian civilization has made so much of in opposition to the 'bestiality' of animals? *Cromwell* suggests a darker, innate and submerged element in humankind which is so hard to face that we externalize it—so that when someone commits an atrocity he is turned into a 'beast'. Disturbing poems like 'An Old Murderer's Gift' (the murderer is an old soldier) tell of the love of killing, the love of seeing fear in the faces of others. Killing, instead of being somehow 'inhuman'—which is how most of us would like to see it—is a kind of unholy sacrament in which humanity drinks its own blood and is fulfilled. A man who has his hand torn off by another, disembodied 'hand' (one of a number of successful *Crow*-like personifications in *Cromwell*) which has 'turned into a meat-crusher', is given blood from his own crushed hand to drink:

135

'I am water' he said, 'Watch me as I sink.
I am blood in this chalice at my lip.
I am a hunter, and my own victim.'

Love of killing is related in the poems to that other deep human drive, sex. In 'The Crowd and the Curse', the curse, another personification—of Ireland's centuries' long interlock with England, but also of the deeper curse of human nature that cannot let go, cannot forgive—is gladly eaten, again as a sacrament, by Buffún. It is, however, a sacrament which when taken by the crowd releases them, and justifies anger and violence in a kind of sublimated sexual drive. A crowd gathers angrily after the shooting of a boy by a Tan:

The crowd splits the night with its need
The curse and the crowd copulate there.

And the curse, of course, is embedded in language and attitudes to language, nowhere more so than in England's dealing with the Celts. A group of poems is concerned with Irish and the perimeter of love and hate that surrounds it. There are those who, in 'That Word', see the language as a political force, a threat to the *status quo*. Those who, like the labourer in 'What Use?', know Gaelic will never get them a job on an English building site and believe it 'should have been choked at birth/To stop it wasting my heart and mind'. Those who hope rather forlornly in 'Someone, Somewhere' that the language can never die so long as someone is alive to say 'it is mine'. And in 'A Language' there is the truth that many in Wales, too, would sooner forget:

A man without a language
Is half a man, if he's lucky.

Such abrasiveness, divisiveness and self-hate over language is something the English rarely understand because, again, they are caught in the conceptual snare of their own secure sense of English. In this, Cromwell is presented as the archetypal Englishman, arguing for the divine right of the English tongue—'the language of heaven'—to extirpate others: a process which is seen, by an inescapable logic, as a liberation for those who adopt it at the expense of their own. Cromwell tells Buffún:

Immerse yourself in that felicitous tongue,
Absorb its magic through proper attention,
Utter yourself, universalize your views.

In a prefatory note, Brendan Kennelly remarks that 'Because of history an Irish poet, to realize himself, must turn the full attention of his imagination to the English tradition. An English poet committed to the same task need hardly give the smallest thought to things Irish.' *Cromwell* was first published in Dublin in 1983 which, of course, is not 'really' to be published. The sequence is an achievement, and now this Bloodaxe edition will make it visible in England. One wonders how many readers there will appreciate the fine irony of an Irish poet taking Cromwell's advice, but using an extraordinary command of English to undermine English complacence about language—and about national identity. The nightmare of M.P.G.M. Buffún Esq. is also theirs.

Robert Lowell's *History*

> About 80 of the poems in *History* are new, the rest are taken from my last published poem, *Notebook* begun six years ago. All the poems have been changed, some heavily. I have plotted. My old title, *Notebook*, was more accurate than I wished, i.e. the composition was jumbled. I hope this jumble or jungle is cleared—that I have cut the waste marble from the figure.

Robert Lowell's prefatory note to *History* reveals his dissatisfaction with the collection on which it is based. He refers to *Notebook* as a 'poem', but in fact it is a collection of poems, and it is at the level of ordering and structure that the earlier volume fails. The sonnet form demands integration into a larger pattern of ideas if it is to succeed at book length; otherwise it creates a regularity of effect which it is hard not to find monotonous. Despite coherences and resonances between groups of poems, *Notebook* succumbs to this danger. His reworking of these poems in *History* and *For Lizzie and Harriet* seemed an indulgence to some critics and readers at the time. Certainly Lowell should have had the critical foresight not to have published *Notebook* as it stands, but the deed done, it was essential to re-order the sonnets if their true achievement was to be realized. Lowell indeed had to 'cut the waste marble from the figure'.

As is well known, he did this by placing the more intimate poems about his wife and daughter in one collection, and by structuring other poems from *Notebook*, together with additions, chronologically under the title *History*. 'History' here, however, is not the disciplined study of man in society of the modern historian. Lowell's history begins with Genesis, moves through the Old Testament to classical Greece, on to the Rome of the Republic and Empire, and then traces the fate of European civilization from the Middle Ages to present times, ending in the America of his own day.

The pattern is interesting. It is reminiscent of the universal histories of the Middle Ages, with their concern to discover God's design on Earth: histories which, like Robert Lowell's, begin with the creation and end in the loose ends and muddle of the present. Lowell's history is like theirs too in his 'uncritical' blend of myth, legend and historical fact, and in his dwelling on the lives of great men and women as one of the prime functions of the historian.

But here the likeness ends. The universal history of a man like Ranulph Higden unfolds according to the design of God, which will end in the destruction of the Earth and the Last Judgement. It is a design in which man has a distinct and preordained place. Robert Lowell's history offers no such assurance. In fact, the Incarnation, that central event which gives faith to the medieval chronicler, and which is the pivotal point in his concept of history, is blotted from the record in the poet's account. The effect is to give the Christian history of Western man a bleak, late twentieth-century perspective.

History is also, of course, Lowell's history, plotting the contours of his thoughts and feelings under the exigencies of experience: experience which includes his sense of Western culture derived from art and history, as well as the day to day events of his personal life. In fact, in the sequence, the one informs the other, and we as readers are continuallly made aware of the play of the poet's mind on our culture's past, as well as the ways in which that past bears down on the present, and on the poet's life and work.

The opening poem, itself called 'History', reveals Robert Lowell's method. History here is order perceived in the process of life past, which like the present is untidy, unending, and recalcitrant to meaning. As a human activity, history 'has to live with what was here,/clutching and close to fumbling all we had'. Then with a sudden shift in thought, he turns to our fate as individuals:

> it is so dull and gruesome how we die,
> unlike writing, life never finishes.

History, like poetry, is 'writing', is the forging of significance out of individual lives, even if each life, separately, ends in a 'dull and gruesome' dying.

The 'we' here indicates an inclusive generality, but there is a strong sense that Robert Lowell really means 'I'; that it is his own approaching death which is being reflected on. Death pervades this poem and, with it, horror and fear. Cain struck Abel, and 'Abel was finished'. The rising moon is beautiful, but it is also 'white-faced, predatory', and an emblem of death: 'a child could give it a face: two holes, two holes'—which merges into the poet's face rotting into death, 'my eyes, my mouth, between them a skull's no-nose'.

'History' sets the tone for much to come, with its intimate voice, its blend of historical and personal anguish, and its suggestion of history as a summation of human terror and horror. For from the beginning of this 'universal history', things go wrong. What is or might have been beautiful or ideal, is lost. In 'Bird?', in a dream, he hears a French voice singing of April: a voice suggestive of the medieval court world of *amour courtois*, with its idealized lovers, walled Edenic garden, and eternal springtime. There is no spring for the poet, however. Instead, in the dream, an archaeopteryx flies up out of a primeval forest, an image of instinctual life-force, a distant precursor of man. As if it is a powerful magical charm, he tries to 'snatch its crest, the crown, at least, and cross/the perilous passage, sound in mind and body'. But though 'often reaching the passage', he fails.

The next poem, 'Dawn', deals with the skyscrapers of New York, centering on one tall, anonymous building, where from a balcony hangs a crimson Harvard blazer, reminiscent of his own when he was a student: 'hollow, blowing,/shining its Harvard shield to the fall air . . .' The poem continues:

> Eve and Adam adventuring from the ache
> of the first sleep, met forms less primitive
> and functional, when they gazed on the stone-axe
> and Hawaiian fig-leaf hanging from their fig-tree . . .

This sudden juxtaposition is an illumination of the primitive nature of our lives in the midst of technological profusion: 'Nothing more established, pure and lonely' than New York early on a Sunday morning. History in this sequence is not so much a matter of simple chronological development, as one of insight into the depths of human experience, whether in the newly fallen world of Adam and Eve, Cain and Abel, or among the bleak, lonely skyscrapers of New York.

In another poem early in the sequence, 'Our Fathers', the fathers of the title are the patriarchs of the Old Testament, but also our forefathers, all authority gone, leaving their heirs to face as best they can the problem of living, over and over. From virus to dinosaur to neanderthal, 'we lack staying power, though we will to live'. Abel was the first to learn this in his moment of death. The poem ends with questions: is there no significance in evolution? Are our fallen lives inevitable? 'Is the Lord increased by desolation?' But there are no answers, at least no comforting ones. In 'Solomon's Wisdom', the King at fifty contemplates with horror toad-like old age. Solomon's songs, his hymns to sensual beauty, become obscene from this perspective; and there is no hint of the spiritual interpretation laid upon them by Christianity. The King is left only with his disillusionment: the wisdom of the title.

'Solomon's Wisdom' is given a deliberately historical dimension. The entire sonnet is enclosed in quotation marks, indicating the direct speech and living voice of the King. This is 'history' in the Medieval and Classical sense, where the historian is free to embelish his subject-matter with speeches indicative of what a character might reasonably have said, or felt, or thought, at a given moment. It serves in Robert Lowell's case to present a point of view ostensibly set in the past, but with an imaginative immediacy and urgency. At the same time, the formal frame of inverted commas, distances the ideas expressed, to a degree at least, from Robert Lowell himself.

In other poems he abandons such historical set pieces and is blatantly anachronistic or presents the past from an overtly modern, often personal, point of view. 'Old Wanderer' and 'Judith' have as their subject Jewish intellectuals and Jewish women, seen respectively from Lowell's viewpoint and that of a (Jewish?) graduate from Radcliffe. The intellectual, envied yet disliked by Robert Lowell, is presented as at ease with nineteenth-century European culture in a way in which he, Lowell, is not; yet the intellectual is also restless, clever, self-assertive, aggressive, hating Jews while asserting Jewishness, adapting everywhere and belonging nowhere. The woman in 'Judith', on the other hand, is confident, dominant over husband and son. Holofernes was no match for such a woman: 'smack! her sword divorces his codshead from the codspiece'.

These poems are decidedly modern. But the Old Testament context suggests how our lives are fashioned by a kind of cultural-historical process beyond our control. The New York Jewish intellectual is only the latest guise of the Wandering Jew of medieval legend; the modern American Jewish woman is another example of the vigorous, forthright and ruthless Jewess prefigured in the biblical Judith.

To accomodate these shifts in stance within so large an historical framework, Lowell developed a style which is one of the achievements of the collection. In his early poems he attempted an ornate style which he could not master. Even the much praised 'The Quaker Graveyard in Nantucket' seems a failure, the imagery too literary, rhetorical and studied; a cobbled piece of work, reflecting the dead hand of New Critical orthodoxy.

In *Life Studies*, perhaps the most famous *volte-face* in modern poetry, he abandoned this highly structured, highly conscious style, for the open, prose-like, reflective medium he used in 'My Last Afternoon with Uncle Devereux Winslow', and other poems in the ostensibly autobiographical section of the book. This was a necessary cleansing. *Lord Weary's Castle* had been a false start, employing a high style Lowell was too immature to control. It was nevertheless, I believe, the style which he learned to approach indirectly and afresh through *Life Studies*. The more subdued manner of that collection taught him how to handle his own life (always his one, true subject) in verse—something which had been restricted, half-repressed, by the unwieldy rhetoric of *Lord Weary's Castle*. Through *For the Union Dead* and *Near the Ocean*, having mastered the most difficult skill of a plain style, he worked his way back towards the high style he had attempted in his first poems: and in the sonnets of *Notebook* and *History* he succeeded.

Critics have responded varyingly to these developments. *Life Studies* undoubtedly is Lowell's most popular and influential collection; one which influenced, and fits most easily into, the plain style that has dominated so much post-war American verse. Consequently Louis Simpson in a review of *Day by Day* sees *Notebook* (and by implication, *History*) as a false turn stylistically:

> Then came *Notebook*, which fell between two stools, being neither imagistic and free in form nor compressed [like *Lord Weary's Castle*]. Some of these unrhymed sonnets were good . . . But in general the lines were loose, and there was no sense that the poems were shaped by the excitement of writing.
>
> *(A Company of Poets)*

Geoffrey Thurley is even less enthusiastic. Writing of *Notebook* he says:

> The sonnet structure of the whole sequence was, presumably, suggested by the quasi-classical form of Berryman's *Dream Songs*: in Lowell's case it seems little more than a gimmick, seemingly intended to give the disorganised jottings something of a classic scale of reference. This is surely the old Romantic agony enacting itself yet again in the wrestle with words, talent and destiny heroically persevered in by Yeats and Crane. But Yeats and Crane persisted with their differing styles, and never lost sight of the end of the struggle, even when they could not have said what it was [sic]. Lowell seems to have lost all sense of the importance of the quest; his style has fallen to pieces. He lacks the strength not only to keep up the heroic manner, but to come clean when the heart has gone out of it: he lacks, all but completely, the necessary frankness, and, yes, the intelligence, to make his confessions interesting.
>
> *(The American Moment)*

Toward the end of *History,* Lowell himself quotes from a similar negative estimate of the style of *Notebook*:

> the last [i.e. Lowell] the most discouraging of all
> surviving to dissipate *Lord Weary's Castle*
> and nine subsequent useful poems
> in the seedy grandiloquence of *Notebook*.
> ('The Last Night')

It is interesting that this hostile criticism emerges from almost totally opposite estimates of Lowell's achievement. For Louis Simpson, *Day by Day* returns to 'the fascinating, superbly gifted poet of *Life Studies*'. '*History,* I submit,' writes Geoffrey Thurley, 'continues the process of deterioration initiated in *Life Studies.*' This suggests to me that Robert Lowell is doing something different in these poems; something which fails to live up to expectations based on his earlier work; and perhaps most importantly, something out of step with the mainstream of American poetry as it had developed in the 1960s.

Lowell must be the last great American poet to have as his inheritance the mainstream of European culture, and to be able to write out of it with assurance. His Classical education, family background and personal temperament all tended to mould him in the tradition assumed as axiomatic by Eliot and, with qualifications, by Pound. But most American poets today have followed the call of William Carlos Williams to root themselves in a specifically American soil. One result of this has been a form of cultural eclecticism which is, in fact, a kind of rootlessness. Poets try to emmerse themselves in the folk culture of the Indians, or in Zen mysticism; they turn to the work of Greek, Mexican, Russian or Latin American poets—anywhere, in fact, except where the true roots of the language and poetic tradition lie. In the 1960s and 1970s, William Carlos Williams gained a thorough-going revenge on the hated Europeanism of T.S. Eliot.

This means that what Robert Lowell was attempting in the early 1970s was inimical to the prevailing poetic climate in the United States, both in terms of its learned, European cultural frame of reference and in its use of a (much modified) high style. Indeed, it is his style, and particularly his adaptation of a high style, that has been most attacked in reviews of *Notebook* and *History*. Louis Simpson is relieved that in *Day by Day* Lowell has 'given up his pretensions as an epic poet and has stopped writing unrhymed sonnets'. Geoffrey Thurley barks that he 'has never had the power or the technique to carry off the grand manner: what Milton sustains over twelve books in *Paradise Lost* and Yeats over whole cycles of lyrics, is more than Lowell can manage for a few lines'. 'Seedy grandiloquence,' sneers the critic quoted by Robert Lowell in 'Last Night'.

These comments derive from a fundamental misunderstanding of what Lowell is about, stylistically, in these poems. Neither in *Notebook* nor in *History* had he 'pretensions as an epic poet'; nor was he concerned to 'carry off the grand manner' in any sustained Miltonic or Yeatsian way. I suggested earlier that the structure of *History* is reminiscent of the unfolding of God's design as mapped out in the medieval universal chronicles, but in Robert Lowell's case omitting the Incarnation which gave the design hope and significance in human terms. Without that central event, world history may appear too easily as a treadmill of defeated expectations, suffering and death. This I think was certainly Robert Lowell's dark sense of things. It had been expressed in terms of his personal life in *Life Studies*, in the portraits of his father and mother and his failed or dying relatives. In *History* he presents that vision on an historical scale; suggesting that the same cycle of dashed hopes and broken lives can be traced through the record of our culture even into the recesses of its myths.

So in the three poems on Clytemnestra, Lowell sinks images derived from his parents' unhappy marriage and his own introverted, isolated childhood. Clytemnestra speaks in the first two sonnets:

> After my marriage, I found myself in constant
> companionship with this almost stranger I found
> neither agreeable, interesting, nor admirable.
> ('Clytemnestra 1')

> . . . my unusual offspring with his usual scowl,
> spelling the fifty feuding kings of Greece,
> with a red, blue and yellow pencil . . . I
> am seasick with marital unhappiness . . .
> ('Clytemnestra 2')

These poems are written in the plain style of *Life Studies*, giving them a deliberately modern and personal tone. Elsewhere he adopts a high style which sets up expectations of a different kind: in 'Achilles to the dying Lykaon', for example, where the rich imagery and forthright vigorous rhythms suggest the possibility of decisive, heroic action:

> Float with the fish, they'll clean your wounds, and lick
> away your blood, and have no care of you;

144

nor will your mother wail beside your pyre
as you swirl down the Skamander to the sea,
but the dark shadows of the fish will shiver,
lunge and snap Lykaon's silver fat.
Trojans, you will perish till I reach Troy—
you'll run in front, I'll scythe you down behind;
nor will your Skamander, though whirling and silver, save you,
though you kill sheep and bulls, and drown a thousand
one-hoofed horse, still living. You must die
and die and die and die and die—
till the blood of my Patroklos is avenged,
killed by the wooden ships while I was gone.

Robert Lowell achieves a faultless high style here; but Achilles' heroic rage is followed by two poems in Cassandra's slightly unstable, slightly neurotic, and distinctly modern voice:

Such clouds, rainbows, pink rainstorms, bright green hills,
churches coming and going through the rain,
or wrapped in pale greenish cocoons of mist—
so crazy I snapped my lighter to see the sun.
Famine's joy is the enjoyment. Who'll deny
the crash, delirious uterus living it up?
In the end we may see all things in a glance,
like speed-up reading; but tell me what is love? . . .

Cassandra's passivity and resignation in the knowledge of certain destruction ('I knew God's shadow for the coming night;/I saw in the steam of the straw the barn would burn./I did not wish to save myself by running') her sense of self-defeat and 'ordinariness' ('I was not wise, or unique in any skill;/not unreasonably, Zeus became my enemy' ['Cassandra 2']) and her lack of fulfilment ('but tell me what is love?') strike across Achilles' unthinking heroics, calling them into question in the light of a modern sensibility and a modern, Lowellian despair. This is in large part achieved by the juxtaposition of styles. Here it is done in a contrast between poems set side by side. Elsewhere it is done within the poem, lines of Shakespearian richness cutting against a plain-style conversational ease, or a deliberate crudity ('knowing that Trojan chivalry was shit' ['Clytemnestra 3']). This is not ineptness as Geoffrey Thurley seems to think. What Robert Lowell has accomplished is a kind of *broken* high style, the perfect vehicle for his sense of alienation and failure within the context of a broken culture, a broken life, which he finds echoed and reflected through the history of our civilization.

For a self-aware disillusionment, ending in death, pervades these poems. Alexander's ambition, in his urge to control the whole world, is really only a form of a search for death:

> A grave was what he wanted. Death alone
> shows us what tedious things our bodies are.
> ('Xerxes and Alexander')

Hannibal's obsession with glory is another delusion, a kind of madness with a petty, sordid ending:

> The glory? He's defeated like the rest,
> serves some small tyrant farting off drunken meals . . .
> and dies by taking poison . . . Go, Madman, cross
> the Alps, the Tiber—be a purple patch
> for schoolboys, and their theme for declamation.
> ('Hannibal 2. The Life')

The poems on Rome are a portrait gallery in the form of reflective monologues and commentaries on lives at the moment of greatest triumph and when beaten into the dust. The collection as a whole has something of the feel of the medieval 'tragedies', or of *exempla* from the pen of a Renaissance moral essayist. So many portraits from Rome, the Middle Ages and the Renaissance, are portraits in the fall of great men and women, high aspirations plucked down by petty flaws or petty circumstance. Henry IV of France 'feared the fate of kings who died in sport:/murder cut him short—/a kitchen-knife honed on a carriage-wheel' ('The Wife of Henri Quartre 1'). But unlike a poet such as Chaucer, Robert Lowell has no saving faith to turn to from the folly and brutality of the world, so that the mood is often reminiscent of the Cumean Sibyl in Ovid's *Metamorphoses* who has lived too long and seen too much, and only wants to die. Even human love means little in this bleak vision of the world. Paulo and Francesca

> . . . loved if one or two days of life meant much,
> then an eternity of failed desire—
>
> winds fed the fire, a wind can blow it out.
> ('Dante 5. Wind')

Yet our lives, so the poems say, are all we have; and if indeed we are 'poor passing facts' as Lowell writes in his 'Epilogue' to *Day by Day*, then it is the historian's and the artist's duty 'to give/each figure in the photograph/his living name'; something which he does triumphantly in *History*. In the poems on Henry VIII's England, Sir Thomas More and Anne Boleyn are presented at the moment of death, together with small details of sensuous experience:

> Summer hail flings crystals on the window—
> they wrapped the Lady Anne's head in a white satin handkerchief . . .
>
> ('Death of Anne Boleyn')

Snatches of conversation, last words from the gallows that have echoed down history, are here fleshed out, and are given a fresh significance, by being presented in the continuum of succeeding generations' relationship with the past: what Wolsey and Froude thought of Anne Boleyn, the fact that More was Robert Lowell's 'patron saint as a convert', summer hail rattling on the panes, then as now.

In 'Epilogue' to *Day to Day*, Lowell despairs that his poems sometimes seem more like snapshots taken from life rather than art radiant with imagination:

> *The painter's vision is not a lens,*
> *it trembles to caress the light.*

'Yet,' he consoles himself, 'why not say what happened?/Pray for the grace of accuracy/Vermeer gave to the sun's illumination/stealing like the tide across a map/to his girl solid with yearning.'

He must have known this is something many of the poems in *History* achieve. The poems about More, Anne Boleyn, and other Renaissance men and women are also about art and are, themselves, examples of the way in which art celebrates, and in the process transcends, the fleeting moments of our lives. So Holbein's portrait of More holds 'the brow's damp feathertips of hair,/the good eyes' stern, facetious twinkle, ready/to turn from executioner to martyr'; and in Cranach's 'Man-Hunt' 'the Kaiser Maximillian/and the wise Saxon Elector' forever winch their crossbows, for unlike life, 'this battle the Prince has never renounced or lost' ('Cranach's Man-Hunt').

Having reached the Renaissance, American readers might expect some acknowledgement of America via Columbus or the Pilgrim Fathers. In fact, Robert Lowell studiously ignores the heroes of the early settlement and only turns his attention to the States *in medias res* in the nineteenth century. This reflects in a way the settled disillusionment of the book. In the context of history, as outlined by Robert Lowell, the various expectations raised by America of a New World, a new Eden, were naive; a delusion which warped the American nation's expectations and inhibited its self-awareness. For Lowell,

147

America was hopelessly fallen from the start. 'Northwest Savage', with its title's sidelong, ironical glance at the Northwest Passage and the search for untold wealth, is about Indiana Territory governor and ninth US president William Henry Harrison. It is a bitter poem in which the hero of Tippecanoe is reduced to a

> selfish little busybody
> expelling Indians, legalizing slaves,
> losing most of his battles with the Savage,
> with numbers anything equal.

For Robert Lowell, the frontiersman and popular hero is the 'savage' of the title, he and his kind moving relentlessly West like a corrosive force: 'No acid ate more/mechanically on vegetable fibre/than the whites in number.' But Harrison is only an *exemplum*. In a sudden shift, his thoughtless and insensitive exploitation of the land is given a modern application which affects the poet and the reader:

> . . . Did the fish leaping
> have leisure to see their waters had collapsed,
> that even Jefferson's philanthropy
> offered a great reward for their extinction?
> Landthirst, whiskeythirst. We flip extinct matches
> at your rhinoceros hide . . . inflammable earth.

Seen from this perspective, America has always been a place of disillusion and disaffection. Even its vaunted ideals of democracy and individual rights are impossible and unattainable. No doubt Lowell's own passing involvement in politics as a conscientious objector in the Second World War, and during the election campaign of 1968, encouraged him in this conclusion. But it is grounded in his knowledge of democracy's failure at other times and in other places. An earlier poem considers the possibility of a republic, 'But it never was,/ except in the sky-ether of Plato's thought,/steam from the horsedung of his city-state.' 'America planned one,' and Melville was 'fixed at that helm'—but with the implication that it had as little chance in the New World as it had in Greece or Rome. Plato's utopia had 'dimmed before the blueprint dried' ('The Republic').

As the sequence enters Robert Lowell's own lifespan, sonnets on public themes merge with more personal poems recollecting childhood and school-days, his sense of being an outsider, whose sexual shyness leads to self-disgust: 'Back at school, alone and wanting you,/ I scratched my four initials, R. T. S. L./like a dirty word across my bare, blond desk' ('Searching'). Socially out of his league, his very innocuousness must have goaded older boys like Bobby Delano, who jabbed him with a compass and made him repeat 'My mother is a whore' ('Bobby Delano'). As he writes at the end of a sonnet a little later, 'I never thought scorn of things; struck fear in no man' ('1930s 6'). Yet at the same time he was learning to see, perceiving that Delano who later shot himself was 'odious, unknowable, inspired as Ajax' ('Bobby Delano').

The elegiac mood of earlier poems is continued here in poems on the death of schoolfriends and contemporaries, like Archie Smith killed in a car wreck at the age of eighteen. Lowell's city had houses that 'date from Warren G. Harding back to Adams—/old life! America's ghostly innocence' ('For Archie Smith 1917-35'); 'ghostly' innocence because lost for ever, and perhaps, because it never existed. Lowell, certainly, growing up in the Thirties, has in a sense never been innocent.

Poems here take up themes from *Life Studies*: poems on his parents, especially his obsessive nagging at his father and his conflicting images of him—comic, pathetic, pompous, failed; loved in the end but not enough to assuage his feelings of guilt; and yet, the need to rebel, to escape the aegis of that closed-in household. So three poems hammer at Lowell's shame at having hit his father in a quarrel. And underneath it all the guilty doubt whether you can ever really love your parents:

> I always went too far—few children can love,
> or even bear their bearers, the never forgotten
> *my* father, *my* mother . . . these names, their function, given
> by them once, given existence now by me.
> ('Mother and Father 2')

At the same time there is the realization that you can never escape them either, for their very actions and mannerisms are implanted in you through the genes, through habit:

> . . . now more than before fearing everything I do
> is only (only) a mix of mother and father,
> no matter how unlike they were, they are—
> it's not what you were or thought, but you . . .
> the choked oblique joke, the weighty luxurious stretch.
> ('Mother, 1972')

Lowell can never throw off his guilt. In a dream he realizes that as he approaches his father's age, he loves him more than ever before in his

149

life. But the father's answer cuts back: 'Doesn't love begin at the beginning?' ('Father in a Dream').

An increasing note of failure and desperation sours these last pages of the book. Looking back on the best poets and critics of his generation, he dwells on their untimely deaths: Plath, Jarrell, Roethke, Schwartz, F. O. Matthiessen. 'They come this path [i.e. in dreams], old friends, old buffs of death' ('Randall Jarrell'). Whether succeeding or failing at their art, they seemed doomed to torment of one kind or another, and an early death. It is all summed up in 'Our Dead Poets', an *ubi sunt* poem for his contemporaries, where 'Their lines string out from nowhere, stretch to sorrow.'

Poems about fellow poets and about his family are interspersed with reflections on world events that shaped his time; the atrocities of the Nazis; Hitler and Stalin ('In our time, God is an entirely lost person'); the evil monsters of the age dying like Chicago gangsters 'with girls and Lügers' ('Words'); the cheapness, the pettiness of the Fascist leaders which it is impossible to equate with the enormity of their deeds. 'Rats' summarises in a horrific way the poems on this period. *'Only man is miserable,'* muses his Jewish conscientious objector friend in prison. 'He was wrong though, he forgot the rats.' And Lowell recounts a laboratory experiment in which rats experience orgasm if they press the right levers. 'Soon they learned/to press the levers, did nothing else—still on the trip,/they died of starvation in a litter of food.' There is a sadness and a desperation about this. Man did this. Yet it seems a parable for man too, in Lowell's grim world.

There is a sense in many of these poems of a civilization in its death throes, and of a helplessness in the face of an inexorable process. Involvement in the politics of the late-1960s only serves to confirm him in this. There are elegies on Robert Kennedy and Eugene McCarthy —assassination, ambition, good men killed or dying prematurely. Here Robert Lowell witnessed the making of political history, something which he so brilliantly recreates in the early sonnets out of the bare bones of Classical and Renaissance power politics:

> . . . We've so little faith that anyone
> ever makes anything better . . . the same and less—
> ambition only makes the ambitious great.
> The state lifts us, we cannot raise the state . . .

This could be an epitaph on high politics in Ciceronian Rome; in fact it is from a reflective poem on the death of McCarthy, coming after lines in which he asks doubtfully:

> . . . Who will swear you wouldn't
> have done good to the country, that fulfilment wouldn't
> have done good to you.

But whether it be Chicago, Prague, or McCarthy in 1968, individual freedom and political change and renewal are brutally opposed. Under such conditions the poet shrinks back into the personal; remembrance of old friends, old loves, old possibilities, away from the defeat of the present:

> The old team have the city. In an open car
> elected and loser stand reflecting our smiles—
> no insurance policy will accept them.
> Disappointed we discover they're twins.
> ('Puzzle')

Yet the personal is no real retreat. There are too many loners, too many losers, people who are scared and unsuccessful, seeking assurance and affection which Lowell cannot give; too many marriages tolerated but dead ('Eating Out Alone', 'Publication Day', 'Loser', 'Keepsakes', 'The Just Forties').

Even his faith in the lasting worth of art is shaken. 'In the Back Stacks', subtitled 'PUBLICATION DAY', begins strongly and confidently: 'My lines swell up and spank like the bow of a yacht', and ends 'everything printed will come to these back stacks'. In 'Reading Myself', he is uncertain of his own worth as a writer. If, like the bee, he has successfully built the cells of his hive, it is both a work of art and a tomb:

> . . . the corpse of the insect lives embalmed in honey,
> prays that its perishable work live long
> enough for the sweet-tooth bear to desecrate—
> this open book . . . my open coffin.

He turns again to his family, whose images have crumbled into death: 'elders once loved by older elders in a Maytime/invisible to us as the Hittites' ('Those Older 1'). In late middle age they haunt him, the relations of his childhood who were celebrated in *Life Studies*, and those beyond his own remembrance. 'Those Older 2' ends with a dreamlike, haunting and haunted image of universal death:

> And I face faceless lines of white frame houses,
> sanded, stranded, undarkened by shade or shutter . . .
> mass military graveyard of those before us,

151

rich and poor, no trees in the sky—one white
stone multiplied a thousandfold and too close—
if I pass quickly, they melt to a field of snow.

Poem after poem at the end dwells on death: the death of elders, of
his family, the death of friends, fellow writers, public figures. History
is collective and continuous, but our individual sense of things is
finite, and ends with our end. One poem concludes, 'suicide, the inal-
ienable right of man'; the next begins 'Is dying harder than being
already dead?' The book ends with poems of an almost apocalyptic
vision: the millions who have been, who are, who will be, all who have
died or are to die . . . Death becomes for Robert Lowell the ultimate
reality:

Death gallops on a bridge of red railties and girder
('Death and the Bridge')

Since our '17, how many millions gone
('Outlook')

horsedroppings and drippings . . . hear it, hear the clopping
hundreds of horses unstoppable . . . each hauls a coffin
('Outlook')

The last poem, 'End of a Year', turns full circle to the lives of kings
and heroes, dead, gone, existing only in art, in print, unsatisfactorily:

These conquered kings pass furiously away;
gods die in flesh and spirit and live in print,
each library a misquoted tyrant's home.

Words in our civilization fail us:

A year runs out in the movies, must be written
in bad, straightforward, unscanning sentences—
stamped, trampled, branded on backs of carbons,
lines, words, letters nailed to letters, words, lines—
the typescript looks like a Rosetta Stone . . .

The typescript looks like a Rosetta Stone, but the line trails away in
dots; this Rosetta Stone is merely confusion, unscrambling nothing,
the key to nothing. An image of heroic voyaging is briefly revived:

One more annus mirabilis, its hero *hero demens*,
ill-starred of men and crossed by his fixed stars
running his ship past sound-spar on the rocks . . .

152

But this is the modern age. Again the sentence, the possibility, trails away in dots, and the poet is left gazing out over the slush-ice on the banks of the industrial Hudson River, turned to transient beauty in the dusk:

> The slush-ice on the east bank of the Hudson
> is rose-heather in the New Year sunset;

and the poem ends

> bright sky, bright sky, carbon scarred with ciphers.

Carbon/night-sky/stars, scrambled, unreadable; nature provisional; the attempt and failure of art to surmount our mortality.

Askans Konung—The King of Ashes

Euphoria at the 1987 Washington agreement on nuclear arms pushed into the background several significant facts: that only a small percentage of rockets with nuclear warheads will be destroyed, while their plutonium will be used in other weapons; that, within an agreed limit, rockets' propellant fuel will be burned up in the atmosphere, releasing hydrochloric acids and other compounds with effects that appear to be unknown; and that both sides retain thousands of nuclear-armed rockets snug in their silos or sliding silent under the sea. Yet Reagan and Gobachev smiled and shook hands for the cameras as the Russian was given the Americans' highest accolade—'He's a great PR man.'

Beneath the surface of the developed nations there is something deeply wrong, which the media rarely focus on, and which may end by destroying us. It is the subject of one of the great post-war European poems by the Swedish poet Harry Martinson—a sequence of 103 cantos called *Aniara*. First published in Stockholm in 1956, an English version by Hugh McDiarmid and Elspeth Harley Schubert followed seven years later in 1963. At the time, the English translation had considerable success, including a serialized reading on BBC radio. The translation has long been out of print, however, and its publishers, Hutchinson, have no plans to reprint. Ironically, in view of the poem's theme, when I phoned Hutchinson to check this, neither Harry Martinson nor *Aniara* showed up on the company's computer record of published books, and few I have spoken to have read it or even heard of it.

There is a sense in which a writer becomes invisible if his work is not kept in print, as happened until recently in the case of Robinson Jeffers. Perhaps the fact that the translation of *Aniara* has been out of print for two decades is sufficient reason for its neglect among English-speaking readers. It is not in the bookshops; it is therefore invisible; it is not read. Yet reading *Aniara* at last, haltingly, in Swedish, its achievement as a work of art and its importance for our times seem greater now than when I read the McDiarmid-Schubert translation in the early Sixties.

The poem is set in an indeterminate future when the Earth, governed by brutal dictatorships and polluted by nuclear wars, has at last been made uninhabitable by humankind. Technological advance, however, means that colonies have been established on the 'tundras' of Mars and in the 'swamps' of Venus, where the remnants of humanity are transported to work under slave conditions, while the Earth recuperates. Refugees are herded into goldondas, space ships accommodating thousands on a single journey, that shuttle between Earth and the planets.

Aniara is one such goldonda, *en route* for Mars with 8000 refugees. What should have been a routine flight, however, is disrupted by a series of accidents which wrenches the ship off course and out of the solar system. Hurtling irrevocably toward the constellation Lyra, the goldonda sends out its signal, 'Aniara . . . Aniara . . .', but in deep space there is no one to receive it and no one to reply. The rest of the poem recounts the attempts of the crew and passengers to cope with their situation and their eventual collapse by a kind of spiritual entropy into despair and death.

At one level, therefore, *Aniara* is a work of science fiction, and part of Harry Martinson's achievement is the appropriation of the *genre* to poetry. He uses to the full, for example, the convention of pseudo-scientific language—phototurb, tensor calculus, genda curves, gopta —to suggest the scientific advances of his projected world. But Harry Martinson also had a good amateur grasp of physics and astronomy, and beneath the fanciful terminology is an understanding of the general and special theories of relativity, the second law of thermo-dynamics and Heisenberg's uncertainty principle.[1]

In fact, he is one of only a small group of poets to have come to terms with advances in science which have changed utterly our concept of the universe. R.S. Thomas, in some of his later poems, and A.R. Ammons come to mind, but most poets avoid the challenge or fail in the attempt. This is not surprising when the difficulties are considered. Physicists and astronomers work with mathematical formulae which are beyond the non-specialist, and even popularizations use an abstract verbal equivalent. The transformation of this into poetry is daunting, for while the scientist tries to delimit words to specific meanings, the poet's method pulls language in the opposite direction, opening words through association into metaphor and symbol.

---

[1] The English translation has a good introduction by the Swedish mathematician Tord Hall, as well as a gloss on many of the poem's scientific and pseudo-scientific terms.

For the poet the dangers are obvious. If he uses, as he must, the language of metaphor, his science may seem superficial or inexact. If he attempts a more precise use of science, he may end up as a verse explainer like Erasmus Darwin. He also has to consider that most readers of poetry will have little knowledge of modern physics or astronomy, so that either way his poem may seem obscure to any likely audience.

Harry Martinson overcomes these problems by using genuine scientific knowledge as a kind of groundswell beneath the science fiction surface of his poem. Understanding the second law of thermo-dynamics adds to the reader's appreciation of *Aniara* but it is not essential, for the flight of the goldonda through deep space enacts the concept of entropy through the experience of its inhabitants. More-over, the casual use of pseudo-scientific terminology by the narrator and crew—a terminology largely opaque to the reader—brings out how little most of us know about the post-Einsteinian universe or the technology on which our civilization depends. By degrees we have accustomed ourselves to living in a world where we think we see, but are really blind.

And this is the great theme of *Aniara*: how human intelligence has made the universe at once more and less intelligible; how science gen-erates knowledge and knowledge a technology which, because of our inherent limitations as a species, will destroy us. It is an enactment of the Faustian tragedy now being played out by the world's dominant cultures, in which humanity itself is cast in the rôle of the man who would know all, regardless of consequences. The sub-title of *Aniara* is 'A Review of Mankind in Time and Space'.

After six years, the community onboard Aniara has settled into a routine organized around the natural cycles and rhythms of Earth. Time is divided into day and night, and people gather in the *samlings-sal*, the assembly hall, to celebrate the Scandinavian midsummer night festival by dancing till the midsummer sun would have risen on Earth. But such attempts at normality founder under the burden of their true situation deep in the eerie stillness of space.

How to cope with the immensity of the universe opened up by astro-physics? The ship's chief astronomer tries to explain to the passengers. Their concept of space from the perspective of Earth was naive. Space is, as it were, *ande*, spirit, which comprises 'God and Death and Mystery' and through which Aniara travels. To give them a glimpse of what this means, the astronomer holds up a delicate glass bowl. He likens the journey of the space ship to the movement of a tiny bubble of air trapped in a flaw in the glass which, if left undisturbed, will in a thousand years travel an infinitesimal distance through the glass. So Aniara hurtles at immense speed through space, yet in a thousand years will have travelled no further than the bubble in the glass.

In the dayless, nightless, seemingly motionless world of space, attempts to create human meaning begin to break down. The ship's commanders want the refugess to *'se sitt öde/i vetenskapans klara ljus'* (see their fate/in the clear light of science), but that is precisely what ordinary people cannot do. Even the pilots who are 'fatalists of the new kind/ who could only be formed by empty space' begin to crumple under the pressure of their knowledge. Watching them when they are off-guard, the narrator sees 'grief shine like a phosphorous-glow/from their searching eyes'.

At such moments of realization, the inhabitants crowd into the hall of the mima for consolation. The mima plays a central and complex part in th poem. At one level it is a giant computer that scans space, receiving signals in the form of images of life from distant parts of the universe. But it is something more. Referred to as 'she', in Harry Martinson's science fiction world, the mima is ambiguously organic and incapable of corruption or telling a lie. There is a sense in which she symbolizes the human unconscious and the imaginative faculty, sources of images which are also 'true' and which surface in dreams, religion, art, but which can be abused and trivialized by the individual conscious human mind.

So the images of otherworlds reproduced on the mima's giant screen can be used as a form of escape by Aniara's inhabitants, and the narrator, who is also the mima's attendant, can store 'good' images to be replayed at moments of mass crisis and despair on the ship.

Because the mima cannot lie, however, she also reproduces images of horror, and in one apocalyptic canto she relays the destruction of Dourisburg, the great city of Douris/Earth,[2] in a last atomic war. This is enacted in the poem through two powerful images: one of a deaf-mute who tries to describe what it was like when the bomb exploded. Just before his eardrums burst there was a last sound 'like the murmur of sorrowful reeds', but

---

[2] The Swedish refers to *Doris* (Earth) and *Dorisburg*, which Hugh MacDiarmid and Elspeth Harley Schubert rework, rightly, I think, for an English-speaking readership, to Douris/Dourisburg. The translations here are my own but I have kept their spelling of these names.

Det hördes inte, slutade den döve.
Mitt öra hann ej vara med
när själen söndersprängdes,
när kroppen sönderlängdes
när en kvadratmil stadsmark vrängde
sig ut och in
då fototurben sprängde
den stora stad som hetat Dorisburg.

You couldn't hear it, the deaf man ended.
My ear was not in time
when the soul sprang apart,
when the body was flung away
when ten square kilometers of suburbs twisted
inside out
as the phototurb* blew up
the great city that was called Dourisburg.

And a blind man tries to describe the glare just before his eyes burned out, and can't:

Han nämde bara en detalj: han såg med nacken.
Hela huvudskålen blev ett öga
som bländades utöver sprängningsgränsen
lyftes och for bort i blind förtröstan
på dödens sömn. Men den blev ingen sömn.

He mentioned just one detail: he saw with his neck.
The whole of his skull became an eye
which was dazzled beyond disintegration's limit
lifted up and borne away in blind trust
in death's sleep. But it was no sleep.

It is said, the narrator continues, 'that stones can cry out', and through the stones of the ruined city he hears the cry of the mute who was vaporized in the instant:

Han ropade ur stenen: kan ni höra.
Han ropade ur stenen: hör ni inte.
Jag kommer ifrån staden Dorisburg.

He shouted from the stone: can you hear me.
He shouted from the stone: can't you hear me.
I come from the city of Dourisburg.

*atomic bomb

158

There follows a psychic collapse of the human microcosm onboard Aniara. The mima itself breaks down at the horror of the images she projects from Earth. In the aftermath, cult succeeds cult in desperate attempts to divert attention from their fate, or to create some semblance of meaning in life—Dionysian and other orgiastic cults worshipping the body, the sexual act; trivial cults like the Ticklers. The narrator himself creates a hall of mirrors where the inhabitants go to dance, to practise their rites, the mirrors giving the illusion of depth and numbers which is so magnificent it distracts people from the thought of their doomed journey. But the hall is only a hall of illusion, the perfect image for the self-regarding, self-referring world which Western civilization has created to distract itself from truth.

With humankind's literal and spiritual home, Earth, destroyed, all endeavour implodes on itself. Even great intellectual achievements have no meaning. Isagel, a woman pilot, works out a formula which revolutionizes higher mathematics. Shared by the scientific community on Douris/Earth its significance would be incalculable. Sealed within an isolated human society in endless space, the great problem solved means nothing. In science as in art, the significance of discovery and creativity is sharing, transcendence of the world as it is.

It is precisely this possibility of transcendence, however, that is questioned in the poem. A long central canto, 'The Space Sailor's Story', describes the herding of people in their millions to the slave camps on Mars where they are worked, tortured and killed. For his images, Harry Martinson draws on the concentration camps of Nazi Germany and Imperial Japan, but atrocity reaches out into our times from Batista's Cuba, Amin's Uganda, Pol Pot's Cambodia, the British in Kenya and Aden, the Americans in Viet Nam—human suffering on such a scale that the contemplating mind numbs itself in self-protection.

In the sailor's story he describes how, under the harsh conditions of the Martian tundra, the only vegetation is an 'arctic willow' whose tough leaves can only be eaten by a cockerel which has evolved a specialized sequence of stomachs. It is a bleak world, but to the sailor's girlfriend, who lives there helping the slaves as best she can, it is a beautiful one—because unlike Earth it is unpolluted. Even its stunted vegetation is a consolation and a symbol of what is left of human hope. Sending willow leaves as a token to friends on Earth she writes:

. . . se, här blad ur andens skog
och det är vårvind här på själens hedar.
Mitt hjärta fylles, ja, ni anar nog.

. . . see, here are leaves from the spirit's forest,
and a spring breeze is on the moors of the soul.
My heart is filled, yes, you no doubt suspect.

The woman finds consolation in this harsh spring, in the midst of
cruelty and suffering, because she retains her humanity in a world that
has abandoned it, where death is so commonplace that it mocks the
notion of a god's taking suffering on himself through the sacrifice of his
son. This woman

. . . tog del i allt
som hette lidande och offerväsen
men nu benämnes mycket mera kallt.
När altaret blev alltför nött och blodat
föll det sakrala av, har man förmodat.

. . . took part in all
that was called suffering and sacrifice
but is now referred to in colder terms.
One would suppose that when the altar became too worn
and bloody, the sacred fell away.

At the end of the sailor's story, the woman is referred to as a 'samar-
itan' who denied herself out of love for humanity. In the poem she is an
example of love which transcends the evil inherent in humankind but
which is nonetheless powerless to change anything. For in Harry
Martinson's vision of our world, good is essentially passive, while evil
is active, aggressive. This is suggested earlier in the poem when the
narrator explains that the mima, searching space for random signs of
life, picks up far more evil images than good, for

Jämt strömmar onda rykten genom rymden.
Av goda rykten finns det mindre spår
ty godhet tillhör inte handlingslivet
dess ljus är samma ljus
                    i år och alla år.

The rumour of evil always streams through space.
There is less trace of the report of good,
for goodness does not belong to the life of action
its light is the same light
                    this year and every year.

160

That is why the Earth has been polluted by radiation and why harsh dictatorships have seized it and ruled it; why in the embarkation queues for the space shuttles, the selfish and assertive shove to the front. Watching all this, the sailor wondered why *'de fromma'* (the devout) never resisted them. But he knows the answer: their 'peaceableness was too great; louts/quickly turned it into eternal peace'.

Harry Martinson penetrates here to the dilemma of the pacifist. If you do not fight, the ruthless and evil take control and you and the peace you uphold are destroyed. If you resist, you enter the world of action which is the world of compromise with evil. Either way the result is suffering and death for the timid and the gentle. So opposition to Nazi Germany held within it the seeds of the saturation bombing of Hamburg and Dresden; the overthrow of Imperial Japan, the nightmare of Hiroshima and Nagasaki; while failure to act condemned millions to the gas chamber, the firing squad, to hanging with piano wire.

Harry Martinson perceives that our involvement with evil is deeper than this, however. It is not merely a question of a polarized good and evil, with the mass of humanity holding some middle ground of suffering. In the days before the mima's self-destruction, the narrator was obliged to feed the inhabitants of Aniara with a 'well-balanced diet' of horror and delight. Even the nuclear destruction of cities on Douris/Earth held fascination as much as horror, because it was watched at a safe distance on the mima's screen:

> *Och fastän mima för Xinombras öden*
> *liksom för Dorisburgs sågs rygga till,*
> *vi följde gärna offren in i döden,*
> *så fick hyena som hyena vill,*
> *att riskfritt vara med om lejonspränget*
> *för att få rysa av sig samvetstvanget.*

> And though the mima was seen to shrink
> from Xinombra's fate, as before at Dourisburg's,
> we gladly followed the victims to their death—
> so the hyena got what the hyena wanted,
> involvement, risk-free, in the lion's pounce,
> the burden of conscience shaken off.

If at times they felt horror, nonetheless 'the atrocities were so numerous/memory retained only the worst'. But even these, known as *'Topparna'* (The Peaks) were 'forgotten/in whatever chasm the others lay buried in'.

161

Written in 1956, these lines are an accurate projection of how mass television and video films have begun to blunt our ability to empathize with the suffering of others. The endless transmission of images of violence and death in films, news reports, documentaries, blurs the distinction between the real and the fictitious. So reporting of the Hungerford massacre merges with fictive simulations of the real event in a stream of images which accommodates a blood-lust we hardly want to recognize: the need to participate, vicariously, in devastation and the suffering of others, which Harry Martinson sees as a powerful element in the psychology of our species. The need is nothing new of course: the organisers of Imperial Roman circuses understood it well. But in Western civilization it has been manipulated to a very high degree. This 'hyena' in us is the ineradicable evil which, for Harry Martinson, is fundamental to the human condition and which will end by destroying us, despite the species' capacity for good.

The tragedy of humankind is that we do have this capacity and can perceive where it could lead us. In 'Hall 7' on Aniara there is 'the Archive of Thought' where a man called 'Thought's friend' is willing to teach anyone who cares, the principle of thinking, and who points in sorrow to

> . . . *en tankemängd*
> *som kunnat rädda oss om den i tid*
> *fått vara i odlandet av anden*
> *men som då ande inte var förhanden*
> *i glömskans garderob blev undanhängd.*

> . . . a quantity of thought
> which might have saved us if in time
> it had been used to cultivate the spirit,
> but which, since spirit was not to hand then,
> was hung in the closet of forgetfulness.

On Aniara, as here, most prefer escape from thought, avoidance of the spirit. Pressaging the Walkman with its isolating earphones and ubiquitous tinny disco-beat, everyone onboard wears a 'Fingersinger' which, held to the ear, distracts the voyagers with endless variants of the pop music of Douris/Earth.

'Thought' is used by Harry Martinson in its broadest sense, however. 'The dry light of reason is ever the best,' wrote Francis Bacon in the seventeenth century; but it is reliance on reason and intellect which has led Western civilization to the verge of the inner death that is acted out in *Aniara*. A mathematical philosopher brings again and again the same question to the space ship's computer, concerning the frequency of miracles in the universe. The computer's answer is always the same: miracle appears to have the same source as chance, so that the same answer is valid for both. The mathematician has reached the boundary of what is knowable through reason alone. For if chance and miracle are equally likely and appear to derive from a common source, there is no way of knowing, rationally, whether an event is one or the other.

The mathematician's impasse reflects our civilization's impasse, where a huge investment in intellect and reason has led to materialist escapism on one hand and cynicism on the other. Aniara's 'accounter', who is only too willing to point out the flaws in anyone's 'minimum of hope', is himself a victim of the despair he mocks in others, for his cynic's shrug of the shoulders is *'ett isigt andens flin/av bitter ödslighet, en världgrimas'* (an icy soul's sneer/of bitter desolation, a world-grimace).

The dry light of reason is not the only way, however. Poets are not much considered in our civilization, but the best of them hold to a way of looking which we never should have forgotten. There is a blind poetess on Aniara whose eyes 'seemed like/the depths of a dark spring, the pupil of all song.' What she brings in her poems, despite the failure of the mathematician to come at a purely intellectual apprehension of the phenomenon 'miracle', is a miracle which is defined as

> . . . *människosjälens lek med språkens själ*
> *och visionärens lek med ve och väl.*

> . . . the human soul's play with the soul of language
> and the visionary's play with sorrow and joy.

This is *'härlighet'* (splendour, glory), which bypasses the *cul-de-sac* of abstract intellectual inquiry. Her songs are satisfying in themselves because they come from the centre of humanity's meaning which Harry Martinson defines as 'the fight for heaven', 'the fight for joy'.

However, this inner spiritual engagement is continually under pressure from the evil which is also inherent in our nature. 'How terrible,' therefore, the poetess reflects, if evil forces 'gather all the selfish and the angry/darkening their path/with hate and vengeance and the banner of malice.' Under these conditions it is hard to 'unite faith with daily living', hard to understand the doctrine of god's sacri-

163

fice, hard 'in one's silence not to think:/has there not been enough sacrificial blood/and why have the executioners not ceased to exist.'

'*Hur svårt att inte i sin tystnad tänka.*' How hard in one's silence not to think.

At the centre of an empty civilization, however, thought and the understanding it brings are a pain from which most turn away; a fact which has been hammered at again and again by poets like T. S. Eliot, Ted Hughes and R. S. Thomas. The blind poetess knows this:

> *Hur svårt för människan att det sanna känna*
> *som en naturlig lust att genomföra.*

> How hard for humankind to feel
> a natural desire to fulfill the truth.

Eleven years out from Earth, those onboard have a '*syn*', a vision. A spear approaches Aniara, travelling in the same direction but at far greater speed. It rushes past, on into space ahead of the ship. What can it mean? There is much speculation but no conclusion.

Almost certainly Harry Martinson derived it from the arrow used by astro-physicists to denote the one-directional flow of time, which makes everything in the universe irreversible and irrevocable. The spear does not veer towards the ship, it merely overtakes it. It is a potent symbol of Western civilization's increasing sense of helplessness in the face of time, that incomprehensible dimension which flows through us and beyond us.

In the previous canto, the narrator, tinkering with the irreparably damaged mima, picks up an image of a woman walking on the shore. She is so beautiful, seems so alive, that she looks as if she should live, and be, forever:

> *Tro inte det.*
> *Den kvinnan är förmultnad*
> *sen fyra millioner år och ingen*
> *ej ens den väldiga kulturkrets*
> *som födde henne har satt minsta spår.*

> Do not believe it.
> That woman mouldered away
> four million years ago, and nothing,
> not even the vast civilization
> which nourished her, has left the least trace.

164

'*Tomhetens spjut*', the spear of emptiness, says the narrator, went on its way. Without meaning in itself, it nonetheless changed life on Aniara. Some went mad, some killed themselves, others started up yet another hysterical sect. 'So we all were pierced completely by the spear.'

To distract Aniara's inhabitants, the narrator rigs up a screen of rays on either side of the ship on which he projects images of mountains, cities, armies bearing flags of victory. These shut out the 'unbearable void', but only momentarily: the illusion cannot be maintained, for 'even the tapestry of fantasy/needs some help from human will'. The emptiness is still there and everyone knows it. The narrator comes to realize that the emptiness of space is the mirror image of his and humankind's inner emptiness, from which there is no escape.

Partly this emptiness derives from knowledge of how our species can plan atrocities with full awareness of their consequences. The central image here is destruction in atomic wars of the cities of Douris/ Earth. Atomic holocaust haunts the survivors on Aniara; it invades their dreams and they wake up screaming. Yet despite their inner nullity and the desire of some of them for death, when the ship passes through a cloud of dust or ice particles which threatens to destroy it, the inhabitants are overpowered by fear, by the surge of an irrational biological urge to survive.

Canto 79 is a short song in which the terrible duality of human nature is faced. In retrospect, deep in the glossy black of infinite space, the voyagers realize that Earth was 'the gem in our solar system,/the only sphere where Life found/a land of milk and honey'. In an imperative, 'Describe', the song says, 'the landscape that was there,/the days that dawned there.' But the song gives no description 'Describe', the song insists again,

> . . . *den människa som i glans*
> *sitt släktes likdräkt sydde*
> *tills Gud och Satan hand in hand*
> *i ett förstört, förgiftat land*
> *kring berg och backar flydde*
> *för människan: askans konung.*

> . . . the men who sewed
> their race's shroud in brightness
> till God and Satan hand in hand

165

in a waste and poisoned land
fled beyond hills and mountains
from humankind: the king of ashes.

This is opposed in the next canto by a song to the sun, which has within its burning depths a pupil, 'a nucleus/which its mysterious vortex/turns into the star of love'.

The source of life on Earth, the sun symbolizes also here the steadily burning light of love which is the only source of human happiness, and which is the antithesis of the active, changeable force of evil. Here Harry Martinson evokes the summer fields of Sweden with their flowers and butterflies. *'Flyktig är lyckan'*, happiness is fleeting, yet

> *Vad förtjänte väl mera*
> *att vi bleve glada och fromma.*

> What better reason
> for being joyful and devout.

But though phrased as a question in Swedish, there is no question mark in the text (as there is in the McDiarmid-Schubert translation). It is really not a question at all, but an expression of loss which wrenches us away from all questions.

On the twentieth anniversary of their voyage, Aniara's passengers crowd into the great assembly hall. Responses to the irrevocable journey are many, but one strikes deep: *'ett ljusår är en grav'*, a light year is a grave. The anonymous speaker goes on: 'our twenty-year journey/is sixteen hours' light-way/on the sea of a light year's grave'. The vastness of space and time set against our species' hopes and possibilities is brought home again. People leave the hall quietly, murmuring *'ett ljusår är en grav.'*

Time passes, and the interior of the space ship shows increasing signs of wear. But that is nothing to the spiritual entropy of the voyagers. A deep ennui settles on Aniara. No one bothers to take the *'klara andar'* (the clear spirits) from the bookshelves; even an atavistic cult of human sacrifice kindles no excitement and offers no redemption. Besides, those who had experienced the atomic wars of Earth 'found the sacrifice here ironically cool/imagined against Xinombra's hot backcloth'.

In the end, nothing can sustain them:

> *I början av det tjugofjärde året*
> *bröt tanken samman, fantasin dog ut.*

At the end of the twenty-fourth year
thought broke down, imagination died out.

Aniara nevertheless hurtles on, a giant crystal sarcophagus. As the ship's resources fail, it becomes colder and there is no light except one lamp at the mima's 'grave', where the last remnants gather. They are compared by the narrator to the numberless prisoners on Earth, who spent their last hours in cells waiting for the footfalls of their executioners. That is why, for Harry Martinson, the human species finds itself, now, at a great spiritual impasse:

> *Ty rymdens grymhet övergår ej människans.*
> *Nej människors hårdhet tävlar mer än väl.*
> *Fånglägercellens ödslighet på jorden*
> *har tungt sin stenrymd välvt kring människans själ,*
> *när kalla stenar stumma hördes svara:*
> *här härskar människan. Här är Aniara.*

> For the cruelty of space does not exceed mankind's.
> No, mankind's hardness more than competes.
> Desolation of the prison cell on Earth
> has arched its weight of stone around the soul of man,
> when cold stones are heard to answer dumbly:
> here man is in control. Here is Aniara.

Harry Martinson believed in the early 1950s that the spiritual journey acted out in *Aniara* was inevitable. It is a profoundly pessimistic book, yet written with a sense of how different things might be if only we were open to the power of love to transcend the world as it is. There is a sense, perhaps, too, in which it was written with a kind of faith, despite the evidence, that such a transcendence might still be possible, and that poetry would play in it a central rôle. That, at its profoundest and most ironic level, is the justification of *Aniara*, and what saves it from the nihilism of a Beckett or a Larkin.

In the thirty years since its publication, however, we have travelled far along the curve he predicted, for our real problem is the emptiness that exists beneath the thin veneer of everything we do, and which minor political, economic or military adjustments can do nothing to change. Harry Martinson understood this, and saw little hope because of the intractable nature of our species.

Onboard Aniara the narrator is one of the last to die:

Vid mimans gravplats stupade i ring
till skuldfri mull förvandlade vi låg
förlossade från bittra stjärnors sting.
Och genom alla drog Nirvanas våg.

At the mima's grave fallen in a circle
we lay, changed into guiltless dust,
released from the sting of bitter stars.
And Nirvana's wave passed through us all.

In 1949, Harry Martinson had been elected one of *De Aderton*, The Eighteen, the exclusive members of the Swedish Academy, for his great achievement in the field of Swedish literature. Also known as *De Udödliga*, The Immortals, the honour must at least have amused him after the publication of his greatest work, *Aniara*.